Chadwick House Publishing

Food Emergencies
A practical approach to prevention and control

Himmat ... S MCIEH
MIOSH R...

Chadwick House Publishing

Chadwick Court

15 Hatfields, London

SE1 8DJ, England

Publications

Tel: 0207 827 5830

Fax: 0207 827 9930

Email: Publications@chgl.com

Web: www.cieh.org

✓ **ISBN:** 1 902423 98 4

© Himmat Rai

Chadwick House Group Ltd is the trading subsidiary
of the Chartered Institute of Environmental Health (CIEH),
the professional and educational body for those who work in environmental health
in England, Wales and Northern Ireland. Founded in 1883,
the Chartered Institute has charitable status and its primary function is
the promotion of knowledge and understanding of environmental health issues.

For Manjit and Maya

The Chadwick House Publishing series on Food

Contents

Foreword

The formative decade for food controls was the 1990s when an imaginatively drafted Food Safety Act 1990 provided the tools with which to build a strong food safety regime. Paradoxically, this was also the decade that witnessed serious food safety emergencies. At the time these appeared uncontainable in spite of the new legislation. Food-related deaths and serious injury suffered by guests at a church luncheon and a birthday party in Scotland shook the nation. The resulting enquiry, chaired by Professor Pennington, identified that inertia, indifference and ignorance had led to this tragedy emanating from a failure at all levels adequately to act. In other words the law was sound - it was its implementation that was flawed.

A Government Minister playing to the camera fed his child a beef product, an image that came to symbolise this inertia. That image was not a transient 'sound bite', enduring to this day in encapsulating all that was wrong in food control and identifying with the issue that has come to be known simply as 'BSE'. It symbolises the breakdown in trust between the consumer, the politician and their civil servants. This ghastly episode cost the country dear. It ruined not just businesses but nearly an entire industry, going on to claim a string of political scalps and a Government Department. The final cost still has to be plumbed, demonstrating that food controls and emergencies are not to be taken lightly. In political terms 'fudge' cannot replace the reality of fact - particularly when the casualties are mounting.

In human terms 'BSE' continues to ruin lives. Those unfortunate to contract Variant CJD are the obvious victims but the 'ripple effect', spreading out to close family and wider contacts, brings home the horror of what may be a latent epidemic. The repulsive practice of feeding animal protein to ruminants has therefore extracted a heavy price and will continue so to do. A positive aspect is that a 'wake-up' call has been sounded to the world highlighting how frail and vulnerable are the links within this complex mechanism lightly called 'the food chain'.

Such crises prompted a fresh look at every issue of food safety under the direction of Professor James. Triggered by the Government whilst in opposition this root and branch examination resulted in the White Paper 'The Food Standards Agency – A Force for Change'. This stressed Government commitment to 'an independent Food Standards Agency, which would be powerful, open and dedicated to the interests of consumers.' The resulting primary legislation put the Food Standards Agency in place and its short record of independence, transparency and strong leadership has brought a new hope to consumers and an incisive, fair hand on the tiller of regulation.

The establishment of the European Food Safety Authority, created on similar lines, says much for the respect in which the new 'UK model' is held. This is underscored by the appointment of the Chief Executive of the Food Standards Agency to the position of inaugural Executive Director of its European counterpart. With controls to be based upon the 'precautionary principle', risk analysis and traceability coupled to a rapid alert system, crisis management and emergencies there is wide scope for ensuring that action, independent of political interference, will protect the interests of consumers and legitimate business within the European Community in this new millennium.

A book that examines this important area of activity bringing together the legal sources, giving practical guidance and colouring the subject with the stark reality of real life examples, is therefore most welcome. Coming at a time when the importance of avoiding, identifying and controlling food safety emergencies has been recognised both at home and in Europe is timely. The subject is put across well, this no doubt stemming from the strengths of the writer who is widely experienced as an environmental health professional working on both sides of the enforcement and industry 'divide'. Readers working within the food industries will welcome its pragmatic and practical approach.

Dr Roland Rowell
General Editor, Butterworths Law of Food and Drugs
Sutton Coldfield
December 2002

Preface

The purpose of this book is to bring together relevant material on the prevention and control of food emergencies into a single publication. It is written with particular emphasis on the practical implications of the law and mechanisms for dealing with food emergencies.

The intention is to provide the reader with a sound knowledge of the issues concerning food emergencies. The nature of the UK food industry and consumer attitudes towards food, food safety and the existing arrangements for protecting consumers from food safety risks are explored. Also, a number of prominent historical food emergencies are examined in order to elicit lessons to be learnt for handling such incidents in the future. While reviewing the legal provisions and the mechanisms for dealing with food emergencies of varying scale and severity, including those at international level, the text is intended to focus on the practical implications for the food industry.

Prevention of food hazards by means of proactive food safety management systems is by far the best option. However, if this approach fails, a food business should be in a position to bring the incident under control quickly and effectively. The preventative role of Hazard Analysis and Critical Control Points (HACCP) and traceability are discussed while highlighting the importance of a crisis management system.

As the trade in food forms a major part of the global economy, the critical role of the Codex Alimentarius Commission is examined, particularly with respect to the prevention and control of international food emergencies. In view of major developments in European food law, Chapter 8 looks at the likely impact of the 'General Food Law Regulation' (EC 178/2002) with respect to food emergencies.

I hope this book proves to be useful to the reader and encourages debate on clarifying the role of the regulatory bodies and the food industry in dealing with food emergencies, with the ultimate aim of safeguarding consumers.

The text should be of interest to anyone concerned about food emergencies, including those working in the food industry, Environmental Health Officers, Trading Standards Officers, food safety consultants, academics and food lawyers.

Himmat Rai
December 2002

Acknowledgements

I am extremely grateful to Dr Roland Rowell for reviewing this book and writing the Foreword. His insightful suggestions were invaluable and very much appreciated.

I wish to acknowledge, with thanks, my indebtedness to the following for their assistance in the preparation of this book: Sarah McGuire (Chadwick House Publishing), Dr Glyn Jones (Chandos Publishing), Dr. Katherine Thompson (De Montfort University), Peter Willetts (Sandwell MBC), James Wooldridge (Mitsui Sumitomo Insurance), Robert Steenson (South Lanarkshire Environmental Health Department), Dr Raymond Wong (University of Strathclyde), the Chartered Insurance Institute, Pepsico International Ltd and the National Police Intelligence Service (NPIS).

My sincere thanks extend to the following organisations for their kind permission to reproduce material in this book: the Food Standards Agency, the Department of Trade and Industry, the Australia New Zealand Food Safety Authority, the Food and Drugs Administration (USA), United States Department of Agriculture, Food and Agriculture Organization of the United Nations (Rome), Key Notes Ltd. Extracts of statutes are reproduced under licence from Her Majesty's Stationery Office.

Most importantly, I am grateful to my family, particularly my wife Manjit, without whose support and encouragement this book would not have been possible.

Abbreviations

ANZFA	Australia New Zealand Food Safety Authority
BSE	Bovine Spongiform Encephalopathy
CAC	Codex Alimentarius Commission
CAPELG	Chemical and Pipeline Emergency Liaison Group
CCP	Critical Control Point
COP	Code of Practice
DEFRA	Department for the Environment, Food and Rural Affairs
DH	Department of Health
DTI	Department of Trade and Industry
E.coli	Escherichia coli
ECO	Emergency Control Order
EEA	European Economic Area
EFSA	European Food Safety Authority
EHO	Environmental Health Officer
EPN	Emergency Prohibition Notice
EPO	Emergency Prohibition Order
EC	European Commission
EC	European Community
EU	European Union
FAO	Food and Agriculture Organisation of the United Nations
FDA	Food and Drugs Administration
FHW	Food Hazard Warning
FSA	Food Standards Agency
HACCP	Hazard Analysis and Critical Control Point
HMSO	Her Majesty's Stationery Office
HSE	Health and Safety Executive
JFSSG	Joint Food Safety and Standards Group
JP	Justice of the Peace
LACORS	Local Authority Co-ordinating body on Food and Trading Standards
MAFF	Ministry of Agriculture, Fisheries and Food

NEPLG	Nuclear Emergency Planning Liaison Group
NHS	National Health Service
NPIS	National Criminal Intelligence Service
NRPB	National Radiological Protection Board
PHLS	Public Health Laboratory Service
RASFF	Rapid Alert System for Food and Feed
RIMNET	Radiation Incident Monitoring Network
SI	Statutory Instrument
SPS	Agreement on the Application of Sanitary and Phytosanitary Measures
TBT	Agreement on Technical Barriers to Trade
TSO	Trading Standards Officer
USDA	United States Department of Agriculture
vCJD	Variant Crutzfeldt-Jakob Disease
WHO	World Health Organisation
WTO	World Trade Organisation

In this book, where reference is made to he, please read as he or she.

Table of cases

Table of statutes and statutory instruments

The Author

Himmat Rai graduated with a BSc (Hons) in Environmental Health in 1988 and started his professional career as an Environmental Health Officer for Sandwell Metropolitan Borough Council in the West Midlands. Having decided to specialise in food safety matters at an early stage, he acquired extensive experience in enforcing food safety legislation with respect to all types of food businesses, taking a particular interest in training. He has first-hand experience in enforcing emergency food controls, from informal action through to the instigation of criminal proceedings for breaches of food legislation. He has served as a visiting lecturer on food safety at Bordeaux University in France and made several live appearances on BBC radio.

In 1997, he left local government to pursue a career in the private sector as a Senior Consultant with Law Laboratories Ltd. In this role, the author advised major clients from all sectors of the food industry throughout the UK, Europe and the Far East. He devised food safety managements systems based on HACCP and Quality Management principles, while acquiring experience in the management of food emergencies from the industry perspective. As an author, he contributed to Food Processing, a widely circulated publication within the food industry.

In 2000, Himmat Rai established Sentinel Safety Solutions Ltd, a consultancy specialising in food safety and occupational safety and health. He continues to serve a diverse range of clients throughout the UK and internationally. Through his work with solicitors in enforcement challenges on behalf of clients, he has accumulated considerable experience as an Expert Witness and is listed in the Law Society Directory of Expert Witnesses. He regularly prepares Expert Witness reports with respect to criminal prosecutions and civil litigation.

He continues to build on his expertise and in 2001 was awarded a Master of Laws degree in Food Law by De Montfort University. He is a Member of the Chartered Institute of Environmental Health and the Institution of Occupational Safety and Health, as well as being a Registered Safety Practitioner. He is also a Fellow of the Royal Society for Health and a member of the Food Law Group, a special interest association of the Law Society.

The author may be contacted at Sentinel Safety Solutions Ltd:

E-mail: h.rai@sentinelsafety.co.uk

Chapter 1
Introduction

According to the Joint Food Safety and Standards Group (JFSSG), a forerunner to the Food Standards Agency, a food emergency may be described as:

> ... an occasion when a food itself or a source of food (such as an animal) is contaminated such that people's health may be at risk, and where something needs to be done quickly to make sure that the risk is removed.[1]

The last two decades have witnessed a number of food emergencies on a very large scale in the UK, from the BSE (Bovine Spongiform Encephalopathy) crisis of the mid-1980s to the Salmonella in eggs and poultry of 1988/89 to the E.coli 0157 food poisoning outbreak in Lanarkshire in 1996, among others. All these incidents proved to be extremely serious, not only in terms of the distress, illness and even death of victims but also when one considers the cost to the wider society, particularly the National Health Service and the food industry. At a time when food forms a crucial part of the global economy, constant media attention devoted to food emergencies or 'scares' in recent years has heightened public awareness and concerns for food safety.

The emergence of a number of high-profile food safety incidents has resulted in wide-ranging implications for the way food is produced, processed and handled in this country. Intense media interest in and scrutiny of food related issues has kept the subject at the forefront of public concern, ensuring that it has a place on the political agenda. Any government that ignores food safety does so at its peril.

Food is a major commodity in international trade and the nature of the global economy means that it is widely transported across national boundaries by land, air and sea. Consumer demands in the West for varieties of food from all parts of the world to be readily available throughout the year have prompted the food industry to develop sophisticated food production techniques, making extensive use of advances in scientific knowledge. Increasingly innovative use of additives, preservatives, colours and flavourings is a common feature of modern food production that relies heavily on such techniques.

The inevitable consequence of greater mechanisation and automation in the food industry has been the creation of smaller numbers of larger producers, distributors and retailers. The emphasis is on high-volume production and rapid delivery to the point of sale, a phenomenon giving rise to global food brands, to the detriment of traditional food retailers in the UK. An example of this change of scale is the application of 'Just in Time' (JIT) technology, perfected by the Japanese in vehicle manufacturing, to food production. Here, raw materials are supplied to the manufacturing plant 'just in time' to suit production needs, thereby obviating the need to hold large stocks of raw ingredients. At the other end of the production chain, the final product is quickly despatched to distribution centres and ultimately to retailers, to fulfil orders placed a short time earlier. A consequence of this immediacy is that large quantities of unsafe food could be produced and distributed across a wide geographical area over a short period of time. This development has an obvious impact on the effectiveness of the industry to control food emergencies, as suspect food is more difficult to retrieve in an emergency situation.

Examples of major international food emergencies include the contaminated Spanish cooking oil (1981), diethylene glycol (anti-freeze) contamination of Austrian wine (1985) and, more recently, contamination by dioxin of animal feedstuffs (1999) originating in Belgium. The last incident led to contaminated meat and products derived from it being distributed to many countries. The speed and scale of advances in food production, distribution and retailing systems, together with the growing importance of food in international trade, has been marked over the past 15 years. So much so, it could be argued, that regulatory controls and mechanisms for dealing with food emergencies have been lagging behind. Although food law in the UK is identifiable in the Magna Carta (1215), it was not until the latter part of the nineteenth century that specific legislation was enacted to deal with food safety matters. Ever since, food law has developed in a piecemeal reactive way, often as a response to particular crises encountered. The UK's serious food scares of the 1990s paved the way for a robust response by government, resulting in the passing of the Food Standards Act in 1999. This created, for the first time, an independent Food Standards Agency.

The adoption of the General Food Law Regulation[2] by the European Community has signalled some fundamental changes to the way food law will be enforced in the future, particularly with respect to the prevention and control of food emergencies. Also, by incorporating some key principles developed by the Codex Alimentarius Commission such as risk analysis and the precautionary principle, account has been taken of the increasing importance of food in the global economy.

If consumer expectations for greater convenience, wider variety of foods, higher food safety standards yet all at an affordable price are to be met, the task for the food industry is challenging. Undoubtedly, this will require a proactive approach and cooperation with regulatory bodies to minimise food hazards arising in the first place. However, where suspect food is already in circulation throughout the food supply chain, robust procedures must also be in place to quickly bring the incident under control.

Notes
1. JFSSG (1999b) Planning the FSA Response to a Major Food Emergency, CP (99)38/3.
2. EC 178/2002 Laying down the general principles and requirements of food law, establishing the European Food Safety Authorithy and laying down procedures in matters of food safety, OJ L31/1, 1.2.2002

Chapter 2
Impact of food emergencies

In order to evaluate the scale and seriousness of food emergencies in this country, it is useful to put the issue into perspective by examining the UK food industry. It is also relevant to establish some key facts about the food industry and consider the trends in consumer attitudes with respect to food. While the structure of the food supply chain may conceivably be a significant factor in contributing to or exaggerating a food emergency, the key to protecting consumers on the one hand and limiting damage to food businesses on the other lies in a clear understanding of how the food industry operates.

Over the last two decades or so, significant changes in consumer lifestyles and the response by the food industry have contributed to a greater likelihood of food emergencies. The concentration of food production, distribution and retailing in the hands of ever smaller numbers of increasingly large companies has made it more likely that a food emergency will affect a larger number of consumers. For example, the majority of the market share in food retailing in the UK is spread between the top four supermarket chains, and a small number of large producers supply food throughout Europe. Conversely, this consolidation in the food industry has also brought about many benefits, not least the contribution to improved standards of food safety made by large manufacturers and retailers. Whether the motivation for such improvement has resulted from commercial pressures or from tighter food safety legislation, particularly the Food Safety Act 1990, the outcome has seen major advances in food safety management systems from food production through to retail sale.

Should safety suspect food already be in circulation, the fact that it is more likely to remain together in large batches, along with increasing sophistication in the food supply system, means that it should be easier to bring food emergencies under control quickly by identifying, isolating and, if necessary, recalling the suspect food.

UK food industry

In order to appreciate the potential scale of food emergencies in economic terms, the following key facts about the UK food industry are relevant:

- Consumer expenditure on household food in 2000 was valued at £55.9 bn, representing 9.5 per cent of total consumer expenditure in that year. This compares with £41.8 bn spent on household food a decade earlier.[1]

• Expenditure on food and drink consumed away from the home in 2000 was £7.36 per person each week, representing 29 per cent of the total spent per person each week, of £25.[1]

• A total of 394,758 VAT registered businesses in the UK were involved in agriculture, food processing, food distribution and food service in 2000, of which the largest sector was agricultural holdings, numbering 239,500 (61 per cent), while there were only 9,488 (2.4 per cent) businesses involved in food manufacturing and processing.[2]

• The UK is the third largest food producer in the EU, with 16 per cent of the total production after Germany (20 per cent) and France (19 per cent). The value of the UK's food production in 1999 stood at 90 billion euros and major food production sectors were meat and meat products, and dairy products.[3]

• The number of people employed in most sectors of the food industry is in decline due to rationalisation and closure of agriculture-based businesses. In June 2000, some 460,100 people were employed in food, drink and tobacco manufacturing compared to 472,300 a year before. However, the number employed in the food retailing and service sector is growing.[4]

• The UK is a net importer of food. In 2000, total imports of food and live animals were valued at £13.25 bn and the trade deficit was £7.42 bn, compared to £6.03 bn in 1994. The UK export position has been considerably weakened by the ban on British beef exports due to BSE. Although the ban within the European Union (EU) was finally lifted in June 1999, France initially refused to comply with this decision and therefore, faced legal action brought by the UK Government in the European Court of Justice. Exports of beef remain well below the pre-BSE levels.[5]

Consumer attitudes and behaviour with respect to food

In order to gauge consumer attitudes to food standards, the Food Standards Agency (FSA) commissioned a survey of over 3,100 people in the UK between October and December 2000. The following key findings of the survey are useful in developing an overview of consumer attitudes to food and shopping habits:[6]

- A total of 94 per cent of those interviewed who had responsibility for food shopping buy most of their food from a supermarket, compared to only 5 per cent who use local shops and less than 1 per cent who use local markets.

- Convenience foods, for example, frozen or packaged fish fingers, burgers and chips, were more commonly eaten than ready-made meals. However, combining these two types of food together means that 81 per cent of those surveyed claimed to have eaten some form of convenience food.

- Nearly three-quarters (73 per cent) of those interviewed had used a fast-food outlet to purchase food, where take-aways represented the most common type of outlet.

While traditionally the UK food market was based around many small businesses that tended to focus on supplying a local area and serve specialised needs, the 1990s saw an expansion of the leading operators in the food industry. The last decade has witnessed considerable industry consolidation whereby many large companies have sold their commodity interests to focus on more dynamic value-added sectors such as convenience foods.

There have also been major changes in food retailing, resulting in market share being concentrated in the hands of a small number of major multiple retailers. The vast expansion of 'out-of-town' shopping centres in the last 15 years has seen rapid development of the 'one-stop shop', offering the convenience of a very wide range of foods and other goods under one roof. The above-mentioned FSA survey findings clearly show the overwhelming popularity of supermarkets for food shopping. The four leading food retailers, namely Tesco, Asda, Sainsbury's and Safeway, are estimated to account for 70 per cent of all grocery sales in the UK. Further consolidation is taking place on a wider front, as illustrated by the takeover of Asda by the US based Wal-Mart and mergers between Somerfield and Kwiksave, which have increased competition in this sector.

Over the last two decades, consumer lifestyles have changed markedly and this is reflected not only in the choice of food but also in the way food is purchased. The increase in the number of women in paid employment, the generally busier lifestyle of consumers and the increase in shopping at 'one-stop' convenience stores has resulted in fewer shopping trips for food. In 1998 a typical British household made one food shopping trip or less per week.[7] This has a bearing on food safety as the tendency is for British consumers to buy food in bulk, which usually relies on temperature sensitive food being transported by car. This can result in such food being out of refrigeration for prolonged periods. Once food is taken home, the continued safety and quality of the food will be determined by the conditions in which it is handled and stored. Food preparation and cooking techniques are also major factors in determining the safety of food. As an indicator of rising standards of living, consumers increasingly eat out at commercial outlets such as restaurants and take-aways, and research shows that nearly a third (29 per cent) of weekly expenditure on food and drink is away from the home.[8]

There seems to be a trend towards smaller households in the UK over the last 20 years. In 1981, single-person households accounted for 23 per cent of all households but this rose to 28.7 per cent in 1997 and this figure is predicted to grow further.[9] In response to current government policy of discouraging 'out-of-town' developments and changes in the make-up of UK households, major food retailers are concentrating on smaller town-centre outlets, convenience stores and forecourt retailing. Also, in their drive to win market share, retailers are offering consumers 24-hour opening stores and the ultimate convenience of food shopping online, from the comfort of their own homes at the click of a mouse.

Research by Mintel into consumer attitudes towards food shows that consumers increasingly prefer fresh produce to canned and frozen equivalents.[10] This preference may lead to faster deterioration in food and compromise safety during storage and handling. This report indicates further that consumers are the driving force behind demands to eliminate preservatives and other additives from foodstuffs. It would appear that the trend is toward greater convenience in food shopping and food designed to fit in with busy consumers; however, due to greater awareness of food safety issues, consumers are demanding a move away from anything that sounds 'artificial' in food. Inevitably, however, there is a price to be paid if apparently conflicting consumer demands are to be met. This has increased pressure on the food industry to develop new ingredients and novel processes, in addition to implementing new techniques throughout the food supply chain. This has the potential to increase the risks to food safety.

Confidence levels in the food industry and government

The following findings of the FSA survey on consumer attitudes indicate concerns about certain food types, food safety, hygiene in food outlets and confidence in existing measures and the agencies that are responsible for enforcing standards:[11]

• When asked whether they were concerned about hygiene in any type of food outlets, nearly a third (31 per cent) of respondents mentioned fast-food outlets in England, compared to an even higher 37 per cent in Northern Ireland.

• Between a quarter and a third of respondents with concerns, did not allow the concern for hygiene in food outlets to affect their eating habits. Those who did change their eating habits were most likely to indicate that they no longer purchased food from the outlet.

• Across the UK, 71 per cent of respondents were either very concerned or quite concerned about food safety issues, compared to 13 per cent who were not concerned.

• Just over half (54 per cent) of respondents spontaneously mentioned that they had concerns about raw meat, while 13 per cent mentioned processed meat or poultry and 8 per cent expressed concern about cooked meat or poultry. Even when prompted with a list of different foods, concern for raw meat was the highest among the sample (69 per cent).

• When asked whether they had any concerns about food safety issues from a list shown to them, the top five issues chosen were:
(a) food poisoning (eg Salmonella);
(b) BSE;
(c) growth hormones/illegal growth promoters;
(d) the feed given to livestock;
(e) the use of pesticides.

• A surprisingly high proportion (13 per cent) of the sample nationally had experienced a bout of diarrhoea or vomiting in the previous year which they attributed to food eaten in this country. Unfortunately, of those who suffered, four out of five people (80 per cent) did not report this to anyone.

• The highest number of respondents (19 per cent) spontaneously mentioned supermarkets as a source of information on food standards and safety, followed closely by local councils (18 per cent). The Food Standards Agency was mentioned by only 8 per cent of people surveyed; however, it should be noted that the survey was conducted only six months after the FSA was created. Food manufacturers were mentioned by even fewer people (6 per cent) as a source of such information.

• The most frequently mentioned sources of information on food standards and safety which had actually been used were newspapers/magazines (42 per cent) and television (42 per cent), followed by supermarkets (37 per cent). Surprisingly, the Department of Health (11 per cent), FSA (10 per cent) and the Government (10 per cent) were mentioned by the least number of respondents. This shows the importance of the media in conveying information on food issues to consumers.

• The most reliable source of information in the event of a 'food scare' was considered to be television (19 per cent), while local councils were mentioned by 13 per cent and the FSA was mentioned by the least number of respondents (5 per cent).

• Just under half of the sample (48 per cent) were either very confident or quite confident in the current food safety measures. When asked whether the government or the FSA should intervene in issues related to food standards, food safety, labelling, nutrition and healthy eating, a convincing 90 per cent said yes. Exactly half of the respondents were either very confident or fairly confident in the FSA.

In 2001, a follow-up survey commissioned by the Food Standards Agency a year after the first, showed little significant change in consumer attitudes towards food. However, the awareness of the FSA had increased from 58 to 71 per cent of the interviewees, as did confidence in the role played by the Agency from 50 to 58 per cent.[12]

Food emergencies or 'scares', such as the BSE crisis, Salmonella species in eggs and the E.coli 0157 food poisoning outbreak in Scotland, have contributed to an overall decline in confidence in the food industry and government to ensure the safety of consumers since the mid-1980s. With over 80 deaths from Variant Creutzfeldt-Jakob Disease (vCJD) in the UK so far and the potential for many more in the future, BSE has been the most serious food safety issue to have emerged in recent times. This is reflected in the FSA survey findings, where concerns about raw meat was mentioned by the highest proportion of respondents and BSE, growth hormones/illegal growth promoters and feed given to livestock featured prominently as food safety concerns.

According to the FSA, up to 4.5 million people a year are estimated to suffer from illness which they considered to be food-borne and around 50 – 60 people a year die from food poisoning.[13] When one compares these estimated figures for food-borne disease with the actual reported number of food poisoning cases, which for England and Wales is usually below 100,000 each year, it is clear that under-reporting of ill health seriously masks the situation in reality. This is supported by the findings of the FSA research into consumer attitudes above, showing that 80 per cent of those who suffered from food-borne illness failed to report it to anyone. Adding this to the E.coli 0157 food poisoning outbreak in 1996 that claimed 21 lives and hospitalised 127 people in Lanarkshire,[14] it comes as no surprise that consumer confidence in food safety has, over the years, suffered serious damage. Confidence in the government to protect consumers hit an all-time low as a result of its mismanagement of the BSE crisis. In the Report looking into the crisis, Lord Phillips stated:

When on 20 March 1996 the Government announced that BSE had probably been transmitted to humans, the public felt that they had been betrayed. Confidence in Government pronouncements about risk was a further casualty of BSE.[15]

Declining confidence in the food industry to supply safe food and in government to safeguard consumer interests was one of the key reasons cited by the government White Paper[16] on the proposal for an independent Food Standards Agency, which finally became operational in April 2000.

Reversing the decline in public confidence in both the food industry and the government will take time. However, by creating an independent Food Standards Agency, the government has taken a crucial step towards repairing some of the damage sustained over many decades. As the follow-up survey commissioned by the FSA into consumer attitudes in 2001 showed, public awareness of the FSA and confidence in its role has improved with time.

Cost of food emergencies

Food emergencies have far-reaching consequences for society as a whole but the purpose of this section is to focus on the cost to readily identifiable groups within society. The most important group is consumers who may have suffered actual injury or illness as a result of eating unsafe food and if they did not, the fear may be sufficient for them to avoid the particular type of food in future. While it is difficult to place a monetary value on distress, injury or death, a high price will have been paid in personal terms in every case.

The cost to the food industry is also very high. This will range from the withdrawal or recall of food to the transport, storage and disposal expenses. All the time that the product is off the shelves, there will be loss of profit. There may be costs involved in plant closures or for relaunching the food product after a recall. Usually there are costs that arise from civil litigation and criminal prosecution. In view of the increasingly litigious outlook of consumers and the willingness of lawyers to represent claimants on the basis of 'no win no fee', this is one area where the potential burden to business is likely to increase. There may be costs to the wider community in terms of declining confidence in businesses, lost working days, investigation by enforcement bodies and treatment of victims by the NHS. As the foot and mouth disease experience of 2001/2 demonstrates, the impact of such a crisis affects almost every aspect of commerce, including tourism and inward investment. The cost of the BSE crisis to the taxpayer is estimated to be £3.3 bn and, according to the FSA, the cost of food poisoning to the NHS and business is estimated to be £79 per case, putting the annual cost at up to £350 million a year.[17]

Due to commercial sensitivity, it is difficult to establish the cost of food emergencies to the food industry. However, from the little published data available, it is clear that the impact on businesses and the wider society could be great; for example, the food poisoning incident in 1985 involving infant milk contaminated by Salmonella ealing caused 76 cases of reported illness and one death and is thought to have cost some £22 million.[18] On a much larger scale, the lawsuit concerning the Listeria monocytogenes outbreak in the same year, involving Mexican-style cheese in the US which caused 142 cases of reported illness and 47 deaths, is reported to have cost over £411 million.[19]

Where food is recalled, this has major financial implications for the businesses concerned. In February 1990, Perrier decided to conduct an international recall of Perrier mineral water after traces of benzene were found in bottles in the US. The company decided to recall the product from the entire worldwide circulation totalling 160 million bottles in order to protect the Perrier brand. Some four months after the recall was initiated, sales of the relaunched product stood at 60 per cent of the pre-recall figure. The total cost of the incident to the company was thought to be US$200 million and as only £500,000 was covered by insurance, the remainder was met from company profits.[20]

Insurance cover

In the wake of a number of high-profile food safety incidents in recent years involving very large expenditure on the part of the food industry, the insurance industry offers a variety of products to cover a range of scenarios. However, this is a very specialised area, with only a handful of brokers offering policies through specialist underwriters. Since the terrorist attacks on the US on 11 September 2001, the resultant retrenchment of the industry is likely to make such insurance harder to obtain and certainly more expensive. In the absence of published data on the subject, it is almost impossible to gauge the take-up of insurance policies within the food industry with respect to product liability and, more specifically, to product recall.

Dowding (1998) suggests that the cost of even a small-scale product recall could be as much as £500,000, when one includes loss of profits, loss of future contracts and the likely increased cost of marketing.[21] There are four main types of insurance cover available to provide for costs and losses suffered by a business in the event of a recall. These are: accidental contamination; malicious product tamper (MPT); product extortion; and product guarantee. Product extortion covers incidents where the product is maliciously tampered with and a financial demand is made, while product guarantee covers recall costs, loss of profits and the cost of the product failing to fulfil its intended function.

Insurance policies may be conditional upon the client taking up the services of security and crisis management consultants, who advise on preventative and protective measures to minimise the likelihood of a crisis. The size of the insurance premium is closely linked with the willingness of the company to implement documented systems for risk management and loss prevention. In the event of an incident occurring, consultants would be available to advise on bringing the crisis under control and minimising damage to the insured, as well as the insurer.

Anecdotal evidence suggests a very low take-up of insurance products to cover companies in the event of food emergencies. Even among large public limited companies, very few have taken up insurance products offering comprehensive cover on product liability and recall. It is estimated that only about 15 per cent of large food manufacturers have product recall cover, compared to approximately 5 per cent of medium-sized companies, whereas it is almost unheard of among small companies. David Nicholson of Beazley, one of the companies providing policies to cover product recalls, suggests that the problem is persuading clients that it is a 'must-have' product rather than a 'like-to-have' product.[22] Tony Cassidy of Cassidy Davis adds that the companies most at risk are those with a turnover of less than £50 million which operate with a single product or one brand name and those which rely on a single major retailer.[23]

From the food industry perspective, such cover may appear to be an unnecessary extravagance, particularly in the currently 'hard' insurance market, where some premiums have increased 100 – 200 per cent, as insurers attempt to cover their losses. However, even when food companies take up insurance, they may find that cover may be extremely limited due to the inclusion of very strict conditions under which a claim will be payable. This may include a large 'deductible' figure, requiring the company to carry its own financial risks up to an agreed threshold. One scenario the company may not be able to insure against is a food emergency, where the food product itself is perfectly fit for human consumption but the company is forced to recall it on moral grounds or to protect their brand.

In view of the potential cost of food emergencies, there is an overwhelming case for food businesses to take positive measures to avoid becoming victims of circumstances that may quickly run out of their control. As no food business is immune from the potential costs that may be involved in implementing control procedures, an insurance policy that offers protection against such losses seems to make sense, should the unthinkable ever happen.

Notes

1. National Food Survey 2000 (HMSO, 2001).
2. Business Monitor PA1003 – Size Analysis of UK Businesses/UK Food Market – Market Review (Key Note, 2001).
3. Confederation of the Food and Drinks Industry of the EU/Key Note Ltd (2001).
4. Labour Market Trends (2001) April/UK Food Market – Market Review (Key Note, 2001).
5. UK Food Market – Market Review (Key Note, 2001).
6. Consumer Attitudes to Food Standards – Final Report, COI Ref. 4695 (Taylor Nelson Sofres, 2001).
7. UK Food Market – Market Review (Key Note, 1999).
8. National Food Survey 2000 (HMSO, 2001).
9. UK Food Market – Market Review (Key Note, 1999).
10. Special Report: Food Safety (Mintel, 2000).
11 Consumer Attitudes to Food Standards – Final Report, COI Ref. 4695 (Taylor Nelson Sofres, 2001).
12. Consumer Attitudes to Food Standards Wave 2, COI Ref. RS250290 (Taylor Nelson Sofres, 2002).
13. 'Food Standards Agency to Reduce Food Poisoning by 20%', FSA Press Release, 28.7.2000.
14. T.H. Pennington (1997) Report on the circumstances leading to the 1996 outbreak of infection with E.Coli 0157 in Central Scotland, the implications for food safety and the lessons to be learned (Stationery Office).
15. Phillips Report (2000) The Inquiry into BSE and Variant CJD in the United Kingdom

(Stationery Office).

16 Food Standards Agency – A Force for Change, Cm 3830 (1998).

17. 'Food Standards Agency to Reduce Food Poisoning by 20%', FSA Press Release, 28.7.2000.

18. S. Mortimore and C. Wallace (1994) HACCP – A Practical Approach (Chapman & Hall).

19. Ibid.

20. H. Abbott (1991) Managing Product Recall (Pitman).

21. T. Dowding (1998) 'Carrying the can', Professional Broking, November, pp. 43–5.

22. In T. Dowding (1997) 'Can we have our cans back?', Professional Broking, May, pp. 30–1.

23. Ibid.

Chapter 3
Past food emergencies – lessons to be learnt

Threats to food safety

Bearing in mind the wide definition of a food emergency in Chapter 1, there could be a very diverse range of causes. In a report by John Godfrey, a Consumer Panel member of the Joint Food Safety and Standards Group (JFSSG), a range of improbable but possible causes of food emergencies are listed as follows:[1]

- diseases from wild or domestic animals which could be transmitted through food or even through xenotransplantation of organs from pigs;
- nuclear accidents or incidents, eg the Chernobyl incident;
- chemical accidents or incidents, eg the Bhopal chemical disaster in India;
- adulteration of food for profit;
- genetic polymorphism in plants and animals, eg through genetic modification (GM) technology;
- accident involving the Ministry of Defence and the possible security issues;
- terrorist activity, eg use of GM technology to manipulate genes to produce agricultural or human disease. In the wake of terrorist attacks in the US on 11 September 2001 and concerns over the terrorist use of biological weapons such as anthrax, the threat of food being used as a vehicle for terrorist activity appears more likely;
- meteorological catastrophe, eg due to major volcanic activity or impact of an asteroid with earth.

While these causes pose a potential threat to food safety, the risk to the consumer remains relatively remote. The purpose of this text is to focus on more probable causes of food emergencies, for which a brief examination of a number of notable incidents over the last two decades will be useful. The following list of incidents is by no means exhaustive but demonstrates a range of possible causes of food emergencies, which proved to be high profile and attracted considerable media attention.

Contaminated Spanish cooking oil (1981)[2]

This incident involved the sale and consumption of cheap 'olive oil' adulterated with denatured rapeseed oil contaminated with aniline, a highly poisonous coal tar dye. It is estimated that up to 600 people were killed and many more disabled over a ten-year period as a result.

Diethylene glycol (anti-freeze) contamination of Austrian white wine (1985) [3]

Dangerous levels of diethylene glycol were detected in Austrian white wine that had been added deliberately to enhance the characteristics of otherwise 'average' wine. Although nobody was reported to have been killed or injured, the potential for injury was sufficient to lead Austrian regulatory agencies to confiscate five million bottles of the suspect wine. A recall of wine, which had already been exported to other countries, was also carried out. The damage to the Austrian wine industry was extremely serious with consequences that lasted long after the incident.

Salmonella Food Poisoning from Infant Formula Dried Milk [4]

Although Salmonella ealing was not initially detected in samples of dried milk, there was sufficient evidence to prove a statistical link between the illness and the product in question. Comprehensive microbiological sampling of the factory where the milk was produced later found the organism in the processing equipment. As a result of the outbreak, one person died and 76 consumers were made ill, of which 48 were infants.

BSE/vCJD crisis (from 1986)

Bovine Spongiform Encepholopathy (BSE) or 'mad cow disease' in British cattle was first discovered in 1986. To date, over 80 deaths have been caused by Variant Creutzfeldt-Jacob Disease (vCJD) in humans and by the end of 1999 some 3.5 million cattle had been slaughtered in an attempt to eradicate the disease. Due to a very long incubation period, the potential for many more thousands of deaths in the future from the consumption of contaminated beef remains a threat. The Phillips Report concluded that:

> BSE developed into an epidemic as a consequence of an intensive farming practice – the recycling of animal protein in ruminant feed. [5]

Salmonella in eggs (1988/89)

A large proportion of the UK's poultry flocks were found to be infected with Salmonella food poisoning organisms, which were subsequently passed on to eggs. In 1988, the publicity was further enhanced by the then Junior Health Minister Mrs Edwina Currie MP, who stated publicly that 'most of the egg production in this country, sadly, is now infected with Salmonella'. In order to bring the situation under control the government ordered the destruction of millions of birds and eggs, followed by expensive precautionary compulsory testing in new flocks. In addition, an expensive publicity campaign was launched to persuade consumers that eggs were safe, provided they were properly cooked.

Botulism poisoning from hazlenut puree in yogurt (1989) [6]

Underprocessing of hazlenut purée led to the survival of *Clostridium botulinum* organisms prior to being added to yogurt and this caused botulism food poisoning. A total of 27 people suffered serious illness and one person died.

E.coli 0157 food poisoning outbreak in Lanarkshire (1996)

This outbreak was associated with meat products supplied to a number of outlets by a single butcher's shop. This was the most serious food poisoning outbreak ever to occur in the UK, claiming 21 lives and making several hundred people ill. The Pennington Report into the incident found deficiencies throughout the whole system of food production from the way livestock was reared through to the point of consumption. [7] The report made many recommendations for minimising the risk of illness due to *E.coli* 0157 at each stage of food production from 'plough to plate', and for improving the means of detecting the presence of the organism and dealing with outbreaks by regulatory bodies. The report also criticised government policies for the apparent desire for a light touch to enforcement and the uncertainty created by the outcome of the Lanark Blue cheese case (see p.44).

With respect to the *Ecoli* 0157 outbreak in Lanarkshire, the most probable cause was thought to be poor hygiene practices such as cross-contamination, where ready-to-eat food was contaminated by bacteria from raw meat. The infective dose for this organism is very low, requiring perhaps as little as 10 – 100 organisms per gram of food to cause illness, compared to around 1,000,000 organisms per gram for *Salmonella spp.* As a result, reliance on temperature control to prevent the multiplication of bacteria by itself is not a particularly effective control for preventing food poisoning. Instead, the emphasis must be placed on training of food handlers in good hygiene practices to prevent cross-contamination. The recommendations of the report were well received by the government and a majority of them have been implemented. These include changes being incorporated into a number of Codes of Practice (COPs) under the Food Safety Act 1990, including COP No. 9 with regard to the risk rating of food premises to take account of the potential risk from *E.coli* O157, and COP No. 16 on the operation of the Food Hazard Warning system.

As a result of regulations that came into force on 1 May 2000 in England (equivalent regulations were made in Scotland), butchers' shops handling and selling unwrapped raw meat and ready-to-eat food from the same part of the premises now require a licence to operate.[8] This includes shops where halal meat is sold, together with general groceries, fruit and vegetables. The licensing requirements include at least one person from each business attending an approved course in HACCP (Hazard Analysis and Critical Control Point), while all other food handlers are expected to possess a foundation-level food hygiene certificate. In addition to the training, businesses must comply fully with the current food hygiene regulations, implement a HACCP-based food safety management system and pay an annual fee of £100 before the local food authority grants a licence.

Trends in Food Hazard Warnings

Due to the commercially sensitive nature of food emergencies, it is not surprising that food companies are rather protective of information on how they deal with such incidents. This is due partly to the fear of embellishment or misrepresentation by the media reflecting negatively on the company's reputation or brand, as concern for food safety ranks so highly in the minds of the public. From the little information that is available, it is useful to observe some trends in the category of notifications issued and the reasons behind the issuing of Food Hazard Warnings (FHWs) by the Food Standards Agency for the year 2001.

Throughout 2001, the FSA issued a total of 54 Food Hazard Warnings (see Figure 3.1), the majority of which concerned the recall or withdrawal of products from the food supply chain, while others relate to the dissemination of information about particular food safety concerns. Food Hazard Warnings are categorised from category A to D (see p.39 for further details on the Food Hazard Warning system), depending on the circumstances.

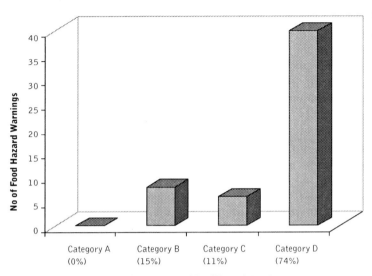

Figure 3.1
Number of Food Hazard
Warnings issued by the
FSA in 2001.
Source: FSA 2002

Category and percentage of Food Hazard Warnings

In 2001, no category A notifications (requiring immediate action) were issued at all and of the 54 notifications issued in total, only 8 (15 per cent) required any specific action on the part of food authorities. A total of 6 notifications (11 per cent) left the decision on any action to the recipient authority, while 40 (74 per cent) were classed as category D and for information only. These figures would appear to suggest that, in most cases, food companies are instrumental in instigating and then implementing the withdrawal or recall of their food from the food supply chain, and the notifications to the food authorities serve only to keep them informed. As the Food Hazard Warning system operates on the basis of voluntary action from both the food industry and food authorities, the FSA may have concerns about relying on these arrangements where it considers that the situation warrants comprehensive and uniform action to be taken rapidly to protect public health (see p.60 for a further discussion on this subject).

Food Hazard Warnings issued with respect to contamination are classified into three types, namely microbiological, chemical and foreign body. However, where the reason for the warning is other than contamination it is listed as 'other'. For example, in December 2001, a Food Hazard Warning was issued concerning mini fruit gels sweets containing Konjac, due to a

Table 3.1
Numbers of and
reasons for Food
Hazard Warnings
issued by the FSA in
2001
Source: FSA (2002)

Reason for Food Hazard Warnings	Number of Food Hazard Warnings issued by the FSA (2001)
Microbiological	13 (24 per cent)
Chemical	21 (39 per cent)
Foreign Body	9 (17 per cent)
Other	11 (20 per cent)
Total	**54 (100%)**

potential choking hazard. The reasons for the Food Hazard Warnings issued by the FSA in 2001 are shown in Table 3.1.

The vast majority of notifications were due to contamination of food, of which chemical contamination (including aflatoxins and pesticide residues) represented by far the highest proportion (39 per cent). The type of food implicated in the Food Hazard Warnings varied enormously from shellfish to baked beans and from spices to chocolates. The food companies involved ranged from well-known household names recalling branded food products such as Nescafé coffee and Ambrosia custard to major multiple retailers such as Tesco, Asda and Waitrose taking action with respect to 'own label' products. It is conceivable and quite likely that in some cases food companies may have implemented withdrawal or recall of food in order to protect their brand from negative publicity, even where this was not strictly necessary on food safety grounds. In addition to Food Hazard Warnings, food companies commonly carry out 'silent' withdrawals from the food supply chain, without alerting regulatory bodies.

Food emergency – case studies
Having considered a number of notable incidents at the beginning of this chapter, this section examines three case studies of food emergencies in more detail to ascertain whether there are any lessons to be learned from the way they were handled. The case studies chosen reflect a range of scenarios and illustrate examples of poor handling through to what is considered to be close to the model approach. The same format is followed in each case to establish the cause of the problem, how it was handled and what lessons, if any, can be learned.

Case study 1 – Benzene contamination of Perrier mineral water (1990)

Cause of the problem

On 19 January 1990, a technician at the Mecklenburg County Environmental Protection Department in North Carolina, USA, routinely purchased Perrier water to dilute a chemical, as it was cheaper and quicker than making their own pure water. The mass spectrometer showed some unusual results and on analysis of the water, minute quantities of benzene, a carcinogenic chemical, were detected. Despite the fact that levels of benzene were less than 20 parts per billion and below the legal limits, Perrier decided to recall the entire worldwide stock of 160 million bottles, a move intended to protect the brand and maintain or restore consumer confidence.

How was it handled?

As Perrier was an internationally renowned brand, the handling of the crisis was very high-profile and the subject of much media attention. Initially, the company tried to limit the damage by withdrawing 72 million bottles from the US and Canada blaming the contamination on a cleaner's dirty rag at the production facility. Later, Perrier admitted that the benzene contamination was caused by faulty filters at the plant and as a result the worldwide recall was instigated. Further investigation revealed that the benzene entered the water when carbon dioxide from a secondary source was added to enhance the carbonation of the spring water. This ran counter to the company's claims that Perrier water was pure and 'naturally carbonated'. At all times, the company continued to state that there was no risk to human health from drinking the water.

The product was relaunched in April 1990, for the first time in distinctive 750 ml bottles and labelled as 'New Production'. At the insistence of the US Food and Drug Administration (FDA) and the UK Ministry of Agriculture, Fisheries and Food (MAFF), however, the company was forced to relabel the bottles 'Natural Mineral Water fortified with gas from the spring' as a more accurate description. Advertising and promotional budgets were multiplied in an attempt to regain the market share but in February 1991 a Perrier spokesperson was quoted as saying that their share of the sparkling mineral water market was 24 per cent compared to 49.6 per cent before the recall[9]. In May 1990, the bulk of the Source

Perrier was sold to Cadbury-Schweppes Group for £125 m. According to Bannister, 'the affair heralded the end of Perrier as an independent company. In 1992 it was taken over by Nestlé, the Swiss food and drinks group'.[10]

Lessons to be learnt

According to Rawstorne, Perrier became aware of the problem eight days before it made its disclosures.[11] The company said that it had to carry out internal checks to gauge the scale of the problem. Perrier failed to appreciate that it was under the worldwide media spotlight and tried to contain the problem within the US market initially. The company's response was fragmented in different countries and inconsistent messages were sent out about the cause of the problem. Also Perrier continued to claim the purity of the product when it became quite obvious that the bottling process involved minute traces of impurity being present naturally in the carbonation gases, including benzene.

Case study 2 – Dioxin contamination of animal feedstuffs in Belgium (1999)

Cause of the problem

Elevated levels, approximately 100 times higher than normal, of dioxins (toxic organochlorine compounds) were initially found in poultry and eggs in Belgium. The problem was traced to animal feedstuffs and it was discovered that the fat added to them was contaminated by transformer oil at the premises of FOGRA, a company based in Bertrix.[12] The Belgian enforcement authorities prohibited the distribution and sale of foods containing poultry meat or egg products produced between 15 January and 1 June 1999. The restrictions were later extended to pork, beef, milk and milk products. The European Commission took swift action to ban the export of the implicated food products from Belgium. As a result of the crisis, the affected food products from Belgium were taken off display shelves in many countries throughout the world, including European Union Member States, the United States, Russia, South Korea, the Czech Republic and Saudi Arabia. The crisis proved to be disastrous for Belgium's food industry and is thought to have cost approximately US$767 million.[13]

How was it handled?

As the suspect food and animal feedstuffs had been exported to other countries, the European Commission took action to prevent products from a total of 416 farms in Belgium being distributed by means of European Commission Decisions. Each Member State of the European Union was required to implement the control measures outlined. In all, four separate Decisions (1999/363/EC, 1999/389/EC, 1999/390/EC, 1999/419/EC) were issued and were implemented by the UK government through an Emergency Control Order[14] and Regulations[15] made under section 13 of the Food Safety Act 1990. On a practical level, the Department of Health sent letters to trade organisations to inform them of the problem and issued the first Food Hazard Warning on 2 June 1999 (Ref: 14/99)[16], followed by eight updates to 1 July 1999.

The original notification and the first four updates were classed as Category D to inform food authorities of the problem but Update Five (7 June 1999) was Category B and required appropriate action to ensure that any relevant foods were withdrawn from the trade. From the text of Update Six (9 June 1999), where the Department of Health reiterated the message in Update Five, it is clear that some food authorities had not taken the appropriate action. Consumers were advised that the contaminated animal products would not be expected to cause harmful health effects due to the low levels of dioxin and the short period of exposure. However, those who wanted to take precautions were advised not to eat any pork, beef or poultry and products derived from them, including dairy products, produced in Belgium. Businesses that may have been supplied with affected products from Belgium were advised to make enquiries with their suppliers to rule out the possibility of contamination or to arrange independent analysis of the products to confirm the absence of dioxin contamination.

On the European Commission's own admission, it was extremely difficult to trace the suspect batches of the food and animal feedstuffs due to inadequate systems for labelling and traceability throughout the supply chain. This resulted in an overcautious approach to be developed restricting larger quantities of food products than was strictly necessary. Criticism was levelled at the Belgian government from many sources for allowing the crisis to run out of control and two senior Ministers resigned as a result. In its White Paper on Food Safety,[17] the Commission cited the dioxin crisis as highlighting the inconsistency of the framework for adopting safeguard measures in emergencies at the time. Until recently, there were different systems for dealing with food emergencies depending on whether the source of the hazard was processed food or animal feedstuffs and whether they originated from a Member State of the European Union or elsewhere.

Lessons to be learnt
The global nature of the food market means that systems for controlling international food emergencies must enable action to be implemented quickly to prevent the risk of injury to consumers. At the time, the system for labelling and traceability of food and animal feedstuffs was inadequate to enable rapid identification and isolation of suspect batches. Also the European Commission lacked a single emergency procedure to deal with all types of food and feed, regardless of its geographical origin. The introduction of new European food safety laws on improved traceability and recall systems, together with the establishment of a European Food Safety Authority and emergency powers being made available to the European Commission, is intended to enable international food emergencies to be controlled more effectively. (See Chapter 8 for further details on the implication of the new legislation for the handling of food emergencies.)

Case study 3 – Syringe in cans of Pepsi (1993) [18]

Cause of the problem
On 10 June 1993, Alpac Corporation, a franchise bottler on behalf of Pepsi, was contacted by an 82-year-old customer from Tacoma in the US who claimed to have found a syringe in a can of Diet Pepsi. This was followed by a similar complaint 12 hours later. Soon after the media reported the story nationally 'copy-cat' claims were received from 23 states. The so-called Pepsi Scare was the top media story for the next 96 hours.

How was it handled?
Alpac immediately set up a crisis management team and established a policy of transparency and honesty with respect to enquiries from consumers, the press and customers. The Food and Drugs Administration (FDA) carried out thorough investigations at bottling plants and could not establish how syringes could have entered the product at the factory. As soon as the incident ceased being a localised issue, Pepsi management took charge. A crisis management team, headed by the company president and

directed by the crisis coordinator, was established. The team also included senior executives representing the key functions within the organisation. The main responsibilities of the key disciplines were as follows:

- *Public Affairs* – handled the huge interest from the mass media. This included the production of video news releases, audio tapes, press releases, charts and photographs to support the outgoing company message.
- *Consumer Relations* – dealt with consumer enquiries on a 24-hour freephone helpline to allay fears about the safety of Pepsi products. Two dozen specialists and 40 volunteers handled 10,000 calls during the week of the crisis.
- *Scientific and Regulatory Affairs* – technical and product safety experts worked with the FDA's Office of Criminal Investigation to track each complaint concerning contamination by a syringe.
- *Sales and Marketing* – communicated with Pepsi customers such as supermarkets and restaurants to keep them informed of the latest developments.
- *Manufacturing* – experts worked closely with investigating officers from the FDA to explain how the product is produced and what control measures are taken to prevent contamination of the product.
- *Law Department* – the company's in-house lawyers advised the crisis management team on the legal implications of the communication and reporting issues.

All communication was channelled through a clearing house and from the outset, the company provided up-to-date, accurate and consistent information on developments to consumers, reporters, their own employees and the FDA through a single spokesperson. Pepsi also allowed the press access to the factory to demonstrate the sophisticated nature of the drink filling operation. The company produced video news releases to reinforce the point that the high-speed nature of the filling process from inverting the cans and blowing a jet of high pressure air or water to clean them, to filling and lidding takes less than a second and that it would be virtually impossible for contamination to have taken place at the factory.

Within seevn days of the initial alert, the FDA concluded their investigation stating that there was no risk to public health from Pepsi products and agreed with the company that the claims of contamination were hoaxes. Pepsi's cause was given a major boost when a surveillance camera in a store actually captured a woman tampering with a can of Pepsi and placing a syringe into it. This footage was transmitted to all national news networks and received massive media exposure. In view of the circumstances, it was decided that there was no point in conducting a product recall. Instead the company concentrated on reinforcing their message that there was no risk to consumer safety from their product.

Pepsi announced that the incident was over within eight days of the first report of contamination. A total of 55 people were arrested for making false claims and the woman captured on the surveillance camera was convicted and sentenced to 51 months in prison. Pepsi took out advertisements in national newspapers to confirm that the product was safe and to thank consumers for supporting them. Although sales of Pepsi products fell during the week of the crisis, one week after the hoax Pepsi sold 800,000 more cases than the week prior to the incident.

Lessons to be learnt
Although Pepsi had fortunate breaks at times, there is no doubt that the success in handling the crisis was due to the professional manner in which it was treated from the beginning. The crisis management systems had been long established and well rehearsed, while the communications strategy worked very well. The public relations function and handling of the media took advantage of the scheduling of news programmes, while the press were provided with what they wanted to make a story. Although it may not be possible for smaller companies to have the resources to produce video news releases, clearly there are lessons to be learned from the way Pepsi managed to get the message to their target audience by the use of media-friendly tools. In order to gauge the consumer's response to their actions, the company conducted surveys throughout the crisis and by the end some 94 per cent of interviewees felt that Pepsi was acting responsibly.

Another major factor in Pepsi's favour was the public support of the FDA in providing independent validation for their message that their product was safe. The most important reason for the success in handling the crisis was, however, Pepsi's clear and consistent message throughout the incident, namely that they considered public safety to be of paramount importance.

Notes

1. JFSSG (1999a) Major Food Emergencies – The FSA, and Its Liaison with Other Parts of Government, CP(99)38/2.

2. C. Doeg (1995) Crisis Management in the Food and Drink Industry (Chapman & Hall).

3. R. Cornwell (1985) 'How the drinks were spiked', Financial Times, 27 July, p. 7.

4. S. Mortimore and C. Wallace (1994) HACCP – A Practical Approach (Chapman & Hall).

5. Phillips Report (2000) The Inquiry into BSE and Variant CJD in the United Kingdom (Stationery Office).

6. S. Mortimore and C. Wallace (1994).

7. T.H. Pennington (1997) Report on the circumstances leading to the 1996 outbreak of infection with E.Coli 0157 in Central Scotland, the implications for food safety and the lessons to be learned (Stationery Office).

8. The Food Safety (General Food Hygiene) (Butchers' Shops) Amendment Regulations 2000 (SI 2000/930).

9. H. Abbott (1991) Managing Product Recall (Pitman).

10. N. Bannister (2000) 'Eau, so sparkling', The Guardian, 17 June, p. 31.

11. P. Rawstorne (1990) 'If one green bottle should accidentally fall', Financial Times, 16 February, p. 23.

12. Short Report of the Standing Veterinary Committee (99/18) – Brussels, 2 July 1999.

13. Environmental New Network, at www.enn.com/extras/printer-friendly.asp?storyid=3687, 11 June 1999.

14. The Food (Animals and Animal products from Belgium) (Emergency Control) Order 1999.

15. The Animal Feedstuffs from Belgium (Control) Regulations 1999.

16. Ref. 14/99 (http://www.lacots.org.uk/hazard/belgian.htm).

17. COM(1999)719 Final, Brussels, 12.1.2000.

18. Pepsi-Cola Company (1993) The Pepsi Hoax: What Went Right? Pepsi-Cola Public Affairs.

Chapter 4
Legal provisions for controlling food emergencies

Here we look at the current provisions for dealing with food emergencies from small-scale incidents confined to a single food outlet to major incidents covering a large geographical area. This review is limited to the public law in the United Kingdom, although it is acknowledged that in some cases the emergency may extend well beyond national boundaries.

In this chapter, emphasis is placed on the practical implications of the legal provisions to the food industry and the agencies charged with a duty to enforce them. The powers available to deal with food emergencies are contained within the Food Safety Act 1990 and the Food and Environment Protection Act 1985, both of which have been amended by the Food Standards Act 1999 to reflect the role of the Food Standards Agency which came into existence on 1 April 2000. The decision on which provisions are most appropriate to deal with the emergency most efficiently and effectively will depend on the nature and scale of the food hazard. Regardless of the type of food emergency, however, according to the Joint Food Safety and Standards Group (JFSSG)[1], the following are key objectives for an effective response:

- Appropriate, swift and decisive action to protect public health.

- Issue of full, clearly presented information to the public, in order to support that action and provide reassurance as necessary.

- Effective liaison with affected parties, including food producers, processors and retailers.

Small-scale localised incident
If the hazard arises from the food itself and it appears to the authorised officer of a food authority that it fails to comply with food safety requirements (see Chapter 5, p.67 for a further explanation of the conditions), he may seize it and have it dealt with by a Justice of the Peace[2] (magistrate or Sheriff in Scotland). The food must be brought before a magistrate as soon as possible in the case of highly perishable food but always within a maximum of two days of seizing it.[3] The person in charge of the food when it is seized must be notified of the authorised officer's intention to bring it before a magistrate and the person who is liable to prosecution in respect of the food is entitled to be heard and call witnesses.[4]

If the magistrate is satisfied that the food fails to meet food safety requirements, he must condemn it and order it to be destroyed, so as to prevent it from being used for human consumption.[5] The owner of the food is liable for any expenses incurred in destroying or disposing of the food.[6] This will usually be by incineration or disposal at a landfill site, the cost of which, for large consignments of food, is likely to be substantial.

If the authorised officer suspects the safety of food but is unable to substantiate this, he may serve a 'detention of food' notice on the person in charge, pending further investigation or laboratory analysis. The notice may direct the person in charge that it is not to be used for human consumption and either is not to be removed or is not to be removed except to a specified place. As soon as is reasonably practicable but by no later than 21 days he must determine if he is satisfied that the food meets food safety requirements. If he is satisfied he must withdraw the notice.[7]

Alternatively, he must seize it and have it dealt with by a magistrate. If the notice is withdrawn or the magistrate refuses to condemn the food, the food authority must compensate the owner of the food for any depreciation in value, due to damage or deterioration resulting from the officer's actions.[8] It is quite likely that perishable foods with a short shelf life such as dairy or cooked meat products will be rendered unfit for human consumption by the expiry of 21 days, in which case the food authority would be liable for compensation to replace the food if the officer's suspicions prove to be unfounded. Figure 4.1 shows the steps in the procedure for dealing with safety suspect food.

If the food emergency arises from the food premises, for example due to a widespread pest infestation, then provided the 'health risk condition' is fulfilled and an imminent risk of injury exists, the authorised officer may serve an Emergency Prohibition Notice on the proprietor of the business and impose appropriate prohibitions.[9] This may result in the immediate closure of the business or the prohibition of a particular process or use of equipment. Guidance on what constitutes an imminent risk of injury is provided in the Food Safety Act 1990, Code of Practice No.6. Significantly, it is the *risk* of injury, which must be imminent, while the injury itself may occur at a later point for example due to food poisoning or a cumulative effect of a chemical in the body. In England and Wales, provided the conditions warrant such action, the Emergency Prohibition Notice may be served by a suitably

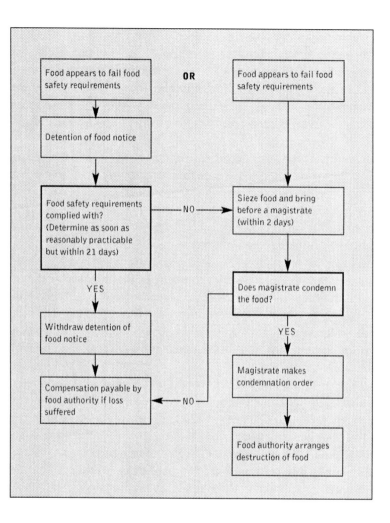

Figure 4.1
Procedures for dealing with food emergency arising from the food itself

qualified and experienced Environmental Health Officer acting alone, although in practice the opinion and authority of a senior officer will usually be sought. In Scotland, however, a corroborative witness is required for the authorised officer to proceed with the service of the notice. Figure 4.2 shows the steps in the procedure for dealing with food premises or processes suspected of giving rise to an imminent risk of injury.

In order for the enforcing authority to avoid paying compensation to the proprietor of the food business, the authorised officer must apply to the magistrates' court (the Sheriff in Scotland) within three days[10] of the notice being served for an Emergency Prohibition Order. He must give the proprietor of the business at least one day's notice of his intention to do so,[11] by way of a 'time and place' notice. If the court is satisfied that the health risk condition has been satisfied, an Emergency Prohibition Order must be made to impose appropriate prohibitions[12] on the business.

As with the Emergency Prohibition Notice, a copy of the Emergency Prohibition Order must be served on the proprietor and a copy affixed in a conspicuous position on the premises. Any person who knowingly (requiring intent) contravenes the notice or order is guilty of an offence. The food authority can lift this order, by issuing a certificate, once the authorised officer is satisfied that there is no longer an imminent risk of injury.[13] If the source of the imminent health risk has been dealt with by the time the matter is brought before the court by means of remedial action on the part of the business proprietor or otherwise, there is no longer a need to issue an Emergency Prohibition Order. Provided the court is satisfied that the health risk condition existed at the time of serving the Emergency Prohibition Notice, the food authority is not liable to pay compensation.

Where the health risk condition is held by the court not to have been satisfied, the food authority is liable for any loss suffered by the food business which is attributable directly to the wrongful service of the Emergency Prohibition Notice. The impact of being forced to close for up to three days wrongly may be disastrous, particularly for retail food businesses. The reputation of the business may be irretrievably lost or seriously damaged due to detrimental media attention or simply from regular customers reading the conspicuously placed copy of the notice stating the reason for closure. Losses suffered by the food business may be considerable and include the cost of lost trade, goodwill, spoilt food and staff wages. However, it is difficult to place monetary a value on intangibles such as damage to brand or loss of reputation.

Practical points of interest to authorised officers
The following list of questions raise important issues and may be of use to authorised officers in performing their role with respect to emergency food controls.

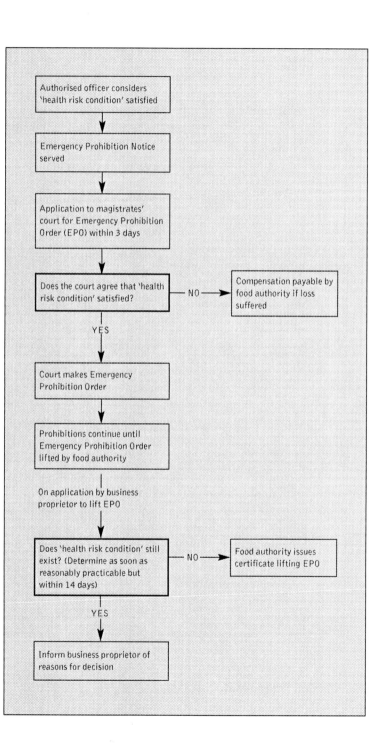

Figure 4.2
Procedures for dealing with food emergency arising from the food premises

Entry to premises
- Do you have a duly authenticated document showing your authority to enter premises?
- Is it necessary to obtain a warrant to enter premises?
- Do you require assistance from other persons for entering the premises or evidence gathering?

Evidence gathering
- Do you have suitable clean overclothing such as a white coat, hairnet, hat for entering food handling areas?
- Do you have an evidence-gathering kit including a numbered notebook, camera, bags with labels and seals, brush, spatula, sterile containers (for food samples), torch?
- Are you maintaining detailed contemporaneous notes of events and findings during an investigation, including dates, times and persons spoken to?

Logistical arrangements
- How would you arrange for large consignments of detained or seized food to be physically removed to a designated location?
- With respect to bringing seized food before a magistrate or applying for an Emergency Prohibition Order, have you briefed the magistrates' court to ensure availability within specified time periods at short notice?
- For large consignments of seized food, is it more practical to arrange for the magistrate to visit the storage location?
- Have you drafted the relevant documentation such as a condemnation order or Emergency Prohibition Order for the court?
- How will condemned food be removed and destroyed?
- How do you intend to affix a copy of the Emergency Prohibition Notice or Emergency Prohibition Order in a conspicuous position at the food premises?
- How do you intend to monitor premises, processes or equipment that may be subject to prohibitions as a result of an Emergency Prohibition Notice or Emergency Prohibition Order?

Serious localised incident or wider emergencies
Where a food authority becomes aware of a 'serious localised incident'

within its own boundary, involving, for example, *E.coli* 0157, botulism food poisoning or a 'wider problem', where food is distributed beyond its geographical boundary and jurisdiction, it should alert the Food Standards Agency (FSA). The FSA will then, in accordance with the Food Hazard Warning system, alert other food authorities as necessary. Food Safety Act 1990, Code of Practice No.16[14] gives detailed guidelines to food authorities on the action to be taken in the relevant circumstances and on the arrangements for alerting some or all food authorities of potential food hazards. This Code of Practice makes it clear that the food authority's actions should be commensurate with the risk of injury arising from the food hazard, as identified by means of a risk assessment process.

Notifications issued by the FSA to food authorities via the Food Hazard Warning will be categorised from A to D, ranked in order of importance as follows:

Category A – for immediate action
These will include situations where the food hazard presents a serious or imminent risk of injury to health or where there exists a possible risk of contamination to other food products being stored or offered for sale. Any notifications in connection with an Emergency Control Order will always be issued under this category and the order may include powers for food authorities to detain or seize food if the proprietor refuses to cooperate voluntarily.

Category B – for action
These notifications are used to inform food authorities of food hazards, together with recommendations for the action to be taken. Under this category food authorities are often recommended to ensure that the voluntary withdrawal of the food in question has taken place and removed from display or storage. Further action may involve the sampling of particular types of food to evaluate the risk to consumers.

Category C – for action as deemed necessary
Where the hazard in question arises from a known batch of food and the extent to which it may be distributed is unclear, food authorities may be asked to take any action that they deem necessary to suit local circumstances.

Category D – for information only
This category of notification is to inform food authorities of developments concerning a previous notification or of food safety matters of interest to them and does not require action at local level.

For notifications falling under categories A and B, the FSA will provide precise details of the action that should be taken by food authorities. While the responsibility for ensuring that a Food Hazard Warning is acted upon remains with the food authority, the FSA is responsible for coordinating the investigation and liaising between the authorities and the food company (or their representatives). Following recommendations in the Pennington Report,[15] later incorporated into Food Safety Act 1990, Code of Practice No.16, each food authority is required to prepare detailed plans and make arrangements to deal with food emergencies. To ensure swift and efficient implementation, Food Hazard Warnings are now disseminated electronically by e-mail.

Since the Food Hazard Warning system began in 1979, it has relied on the voluntary cooperation of food companies and food authorities. However, while food authorities must have regard to the provisions of Code of Practice No.16,[16] they are not under a legal obligation to act unless directed to do so by a Minister.[17] It is conceivable, therefore, that at times, the actions stipulated in the notifications from the FSA may not be implemented uniformly and consistently across the United Kingdom if individual food authorities choose not to act on the Food Hazard Warning for a variety of reasons. Authorised officers may decide that an assessment of the local circumstances does not warrant action or a shortage of available resources to a food authority may challenge the viability of action. This concern was one of the key reasons behind the government's decision to make the first ever Emergency Control Order[18] under section 13 of the Food Safety Act 1990 in May 1998, as discussed on page 59.

In exceptional cases, individual food authorities may be faced with a proprietor of a food business who, for perfectly valid reasons, refuses to surrender the suspect food voluntarily and the only course of action open to authorised officers is to seize it and bring it before a JP. Before the owner of the suspect food, which may amount to a large consignment, surrenders it voluntarily, he must consider very carefully what redress is available to cover the potentially high cost. If the food is being withdrawn or recalled by the supplier or manufacturer, the cost and any associated reasonable losses will invariably be covered by the company initiating the action. If, however, the cost is to be borne entirely by the food business approached by the authorised officer, regardless of the owner's wish to cooperate, due consideration must be given to refusal to take voluntary action on commercial grounds. If the food authority then exercises powers under section 9 of the Food Safety Act 1990 to detain or seize the food, the onus is on the authority to prove that the food fails to meet food safety requirements, before a J P.

In cases where the food authority is acting on a notification under the Food Hazard Warning system, clearly its authorised officer would need to produce sufficient evidence before the J P to prove that the particular food in question fails to meet food safety requirements. Where the cause of the hazard is not readily detectable, for example contamination by pathogens or possibly chemicals, this may require the food authority to obtain its own independent scientific evidence, from a Public Analyst or a Food Examiner, which may take a number of days. This delay will inevitably frustrate the Food Standards Agency's attempts to remove the risk of injury to consumers as quickly as possible.

Some food authorities have, in the past, been reluctant to serve an Emergency Prohibition Notice on the proprietor of a food business for fear of failing to justify the onerous 'imminent health risk' condition before the magistrates' court. This was criticised by the Pennington inquiry[19] into the *E. coli* 0157 outbreak in Lanarkshire in 1996. This outbreak occurred a year after the Lanark Blue case (see p. 44) and the Sheriff's decision to award compensation to the food business was considered, by the inquiry, to be a factor in the local authority's hesitant use of emergency powers to control the situation as it was developing. In a proposed revision of the Food Safety Act 1990, Code of Practice No.6 (1999), the government consulted interested parties on clarifying the degree of proof an authorised officer needs to substantiate in court a decision to prohibit the operation of a food business or a process. However, the revised document has not been issued to date.

The 1990 Act provides default powers under section 42(1). Where a food authority fails to discharge any duty imposed by or under the Act and this affects the general interests of food consumers, the Minister may make an order empowering another food authority or one of his officers to act instead. As time is a critical factor in any food emergency, the default powers and the provisions under section 6(3) of the 1990 Act to appoint an alternative body to discharge the powers are of little practical use. Relying almost entirely on voluntary actions by food authorities and industry to deal with emergency situations on the one hand and on the issuing of emergency orders or the instigation of default powers on the other amounts to an 'all or nothing' approach to the legal provisions for dealing with food emergencies. Where a food authority fails to act and injury results to consumers, it may face civil action by the injured parties for negligence.

Major emergencies concerning food, food sources or contact materials

If the emergency concerns food, food sources or contact material which may involve 'imminent risk of injury to health' over a wide geographical area, the Secretary of State or the Food Standards Agency (FSA) by arrangement with the Secretary of State may make an Emergency Control Order (ECO), prohibiting the carrying out of commercial operations.[20] Where the FSA is exercising a power under this arrangement, actions taken (or omitted) will be treated as if they were taken (or omitted) by the Secretary of State. The purpose of this provision is to enable the Secretary of State to deal with large-scale food hazards where powers under section 9 of the Food Safety Act 1990 are considered to be inadequate. This provision gives the Secretary of State wide discretionary powers to make orders and allow exceptions, both with and without conditions, from any prohibitions imposed by the ECO.[21]

On 20 May 1998, Tessa Jowell MP, then Minister for Public Health, implemented for the first time a power available to Ministers since January 1991 in making the Food (Cheese) (Emergency Control) Order 1998.[22] This was in response to concerns over the safety of Caerphilly-type cheese produced by Ducketts and Co Ltd, as it was suspected to be the cause of *E.coli* O157 food poisoning in a 12-year-old boy. Since then many such orders have been made under this provision, for example with respect to peanuts from Egypt.[23]

In addition to the 1990 Act, the Food and Environment Protection Act 1985 provides the Secretary of State or the Food Standards Agency (FSA) by arrangement with the Secretary of State (designating authority) with wide-ranging powers to deal with food emergencies. These empower the designating authority to impose emergency prohibitions within a designated area, where, in the designating authority's opinion, there exist or may exist circumstances which are likely to create a hazard to human health through consumption of food.[24] This covers food from a wide range of sources, including the land and the sea within British fishery limits and food derived from anything in such an area, that is or may become unsuitable for human consumption. This Act extends to food derived from any creature that has eaten suspect feeding stuff and to anything from which the feeding stuff itself was derived.

Examples include an emergency order placing a prohibition on the marketing of sheep exposed to radiation from eating contaminated grass within designated areas of North Wales, Cumbria and Scotland following the Chernobyl nuclear disaster in 1991.[25] The powers have also been used to prohibit fishing in certain areas off the coast of Eastern Scotland and the sale of shellfish caught in such areas,[26] due to outbreaks of paralytic shellfish poisoning. In this case, the hazard to human health resulted from the presence of a toxin in the shellfish that may cause extremely serious symptoms, from numbness of the mouth through to paralysis of limbs and sometimes the respiratory system.

Once again the designating authority is given wide powers of discretion, as it may do anything which appears to the designating authority to be necessary or expedient for the purpose of preventing human consumption of food which the designating authority believes, on reasonable grounds, is or may be, or may become, unsuitable for human consumption.[27] An emergency order may prohibit:

- agricultural activities;
- the gathering and picking of wild plants;
- the slaughter of creatures;
- fishing for and taking fish; and
- the preparation and processing for supply to purchasers or others of food and anything from which food could be derived.

The designating authority may authorise exceptions to the emergency order and give directions, as it considers appropriate, for example allowing the movement of the affected food in pursuance of the order. Further, it may also appoint officers, who are normally authorised officers from food authorities, to carry out investigations and enforcement on the designating authority's behalf. The emergency order made by Statutory Instrument must be laid before Parliament and becomes effective immediately. However, it lapses automatically after 28 days unless it is approved by both Houses of Parliament before the end of this period. The Act makes provisions for the designating authority to impose additional prohibitions by way of a Statutory Instrument, provided a draft of the order has again been laid before and approved by resolution of each House of Parliament.

As with section 13 of the 1990 Act, any person who knowingly contravenes an emergency order is guilty of an offence. As there is no impediment to orders being made consecutively without reverting back to Parliament, this raises questions about the accountability of Ministers in such cases. This, together with the wide-ranging discretionary powers available, leaves open the possibility of abuse of power and allegations that Ministers acted ultra vires (outside of their powers).

Impact of the Lanark Blue cheese case

In this case, Clydesdale District Council officers detained and subsequently seized approximately 800 kg of Lanark Blue cheese (a semi-hard/soft cheese made from unpasteurised ewes milk), samples of which were found to contain large numbers of *Listeria monocytogenes* bacteria. On 3 March 1995, the cheese was condemned as unfit for human consumption by a justice of the peace (JP) and ordered to be destroyed, and for any costs of disposal to be defrayed by its owner. The owner of the food, Mr Errington, petitioned the Outer House of the Court of Session for a judicial review of this decision and the application for a first hearing came before Lord Ordinary Weir. The decision of Clydesdale District Council to bring the application for condemnation of the cheese before a lay JP instead of an experienced Sheriff was criticised by the Lord Ordinary in view of the complex issues involved. On 28 April 1995, the Lord Ordinary sustained the petitioner's plea in law and pronounced decree of reduction, resulting in the JP's decision being overturned. The principal reason for the Lord Ordinary's decision was that, in refusing to allow the petitioner's senior counsel to cross-examine the food authority's witnesses and only allowing any questions to be put to witnesses through her, the JP had denied natural justice to prevail. The matter was referred to be heard before a Sheriff. However, the food authority and the authorised officer appealed against this judgment, by way of a reclaiming motion.

The reclaiming motion was heard on 8/9 June 1995 before Lord President Hope and Lords Allanbridge and Clyde of the First Division (Inner House of the Court of Session).[28] After considering the matter in depth, the reclaiming motion was refused on 16 June 1995 and the key elements of the basis for this judgment are as follows:

- The duty on a JP to act fairly and to act in accordance with the principles of natural justice are both expressions of the same concept, therefore, in view of the nature of the proceedings, the justice was under a duty to have regard to the principles of natural justice.
- A JP is under a duty to have regard to the principles of natural justice irrespective of whether he is acting in a judicial or administrative capacity. Also, the role of a JP in Scotland differs to that in England, in that a single justice can act judicially.
- The decision to allow cross-examination is not at the discretion of a JP and, in order for the proceedings to be fair, the justice should have allowed cross-examination of witnesses.
- As there was a difference in opinion between the expert witnesses on points which were crucial to the sound determination of the case and the petitioner had been denied the opportunity to test the food authority's experts by cross-examination, he had been prejudiced.

Before the Sheriff, Mr J. Douglas Allan, of the Sheriffdom of South Strathclyde, Dumfries and Galloway at Lanark, Clydesdale District Council (applicant) once again made an application under section 9 of the Food Safety Act 1990 against Humphrey Errington (trading as HJ Errington and Co) (respondent) for 44 batches of Lanark Blue cheese to be condemned, for failing to comply with food safety requirements. The Sheriff heard evidence over 19 days between 14 August and 31 October 1995 and many witnesses were called by both parties. The proceedings were neither criminal nor civil in nature, as the Sheriff presiding over the case was doing so in an administrative capacity. The key areas of contention were whether the particular strain of *Listeria monocytogenes* (serovar 3a) was pathogenic (capable of producing disease) to humans and the discrepancy in the results of sampling by the food authority and Mr Errington.

On the first point, the applicant relied on written guidelines from the Public Health Laboratory Service (PHLS) suggesting that contamination by *Listeria monocytogenes* above 1,000 organisms per gram of food was 'unacceptable: potentially hazardous' and all 44 batches of cheese sampled exceeded this level. In addition, they relied on written and oral evidence from experts in the field of microbiology and on draft regulations (subsequently enacted on 15 June 1995 as the Dairy Products (Hygiene) (Scotland) Regulations 1995) to implement EC Directive 92/46/EEC, which set a standard that Listeria monocytogenes should be absent in a 25 gram sample of cheese other than hard cheese. It should be noted, however, that the UK government inserted a temporary derogation for products with 'traditional characteristics', as provided for under the directive, but the term 'traditional' was not defined. In the absence of specific scientific evidence to prove that the particular strain of *Listeria monocytogenes* was pathogenic, the Sheriff refused to accept the applicant's submission that the contaminated cheese was injurious to health.

On the second point, as there was considerable discrepancy between sampling results from the two parties, the Sheriff cast doubts over the accuracy of the results from samples taken by the applicant and questioned the actual techniques used by the laboratory. In his report into the case, the Sheriff stated:

> In the light of the evidence which I have heard, I was not satisfied that the SAC [Scottish Agriculture College] results were credible and I did not feel able to rely upon them.[29]

On hearing the evidence in detail, the Sheriff found in Mr Errington's favour. As the cheese by this time had no commercial value, he awarded full compensation and costs against the food authority, estimated to be around £260,000.

Subsequent to this judgment, in a report by the Royal Environmental Health Institute of Scotland, the following guidance was issued to food authorities in Scotland:

... instances which a food authority believes may become complex, the authority should consider using a Sheriff rather than a JP under, ie section 9.[30]

In April 1996, a joint report (unpublished) was produced by Dr Syed, Consultant in Public Health Medicine at Lanarkshire Health Board, and Mr Robert Steenson, Principal Environmental Health Officer at Clydesdale District Council, providing a detailed analysis of the case and raising concerns about the Sheriff's decision. In particular, questions were raised about the liability of food authorities to pay compensation to businesses, despite following government guidance issued in the Codes of Practice under the Food safety Act 1990. The case attracted considerable interest from the media and Mr Errington had the support of some national newspapers, as well as some sections of the business community. Indeed, Mr Errington kept his supporters informed of progress of the case and the judgment, by means of the World Wide Web.[31]

Clearly, the Lanark Blue case had implications for the enforcement of the Food Safety Act 1990 by food authorities throughout the UK. From the food authority's perspective, any action taken by their officers has to be justified to elected local representatives. In view of the Sheriff's decision in the Lanark Blue case in 1995, the possible liability for paying compensation to food businesses has proved to be a significant factor in deterring food authorities from instigating emergency food controls.

Enforcement powers available to food authorities and authorised officers

The provisions of the Food Safety Act 1990 are enforced and executed by food authorities and authorised officers (appointed under section 5) within their area. An authorised officer is any person who is authorised in writing by the food authority. Authorised officers are usually Environmental Health Officers, Trading Standards Officers or Technical Officers with appropriate qualifications, but may include public analysts, food examiners and officials from the Public Health Laboratory Service, the Food Standards Agency or the Department of Health.

Officers from food authorities may also be authorised by a designating authority as 'investigating officers' or 'enforcement officers' with respect to the Food and Environment Protection Act 1985. Such officers may then exercise specific powers for which they are authorised beyond the area of their employing food authority, including power of entry with respect to land or vehicles, British vessels or aircraft, etc. wherever they may be and foreign vessels or aircraft within UK controlled waters. Other powers may relate to carrying out investigations in order to ascertain whether the conditions may exist to warrant the making of an emergency order under the 1985 Act and, once such an order is in force, to ensure that the prohibitions imposed are being complied with within the designated area. An investigating officer or an enforcement officer is empowered to seize 'things' for the purpose of performing his functions under the Act. The key enforcement powers with respect to food emergencies under the Food Safety Act 1990 include the following.

Powers of entry [32]

Extensive powers are available to an authorised officer from an enforcement authority, who, if so requested, produces a duly authenticated document confirming his authority, to enter premises at any reasonable time. While such an officer may enter any premises within the authority's area, including private dwelling houses, to ascertain whether there 'is' or 'has been' any contravention of the Act or any subordinate legislation made under it, this power is limited to business premises only and to ascertaining whether there 'is' any such contravention outside the authority's area. In order to enter private dwelling houses, the officer must give at least 24 hours' notice to the occupier of his intention to do so.

Where entry to premises has been refused or a refusal is apprehended and the occupier has been given notice of the intention to apply for a warrant, an officer may apply to a magistrate for a warrant to enter the premises. Application for admission or the giving of such a notice is not necessary if this defeats the object of entry or if the case is one of urgency. An application for a warrant may also be made if the premises are unoccupied or the occupier is temporarily absent. The warrant remains in force for a month and may authorise the officer to enter, if need be by reasonable force. The officer may take with him other persons for assistance, such as police officers or locksmiths in the case of forced entry, but must ensure, on completion of the task, that the premises are left in the same condition of security as he found them.

Powers to require assistance or information [33]

With respect to the investigation powers of authorised officers both within and outside of their employing authority's area, the case of *Walkers Snack Foods* v. *Coventry City Council* [34] offers some clarification. Briefly, the background to the case is that Environmental Health Officers from Coventry City Council were investigating a complaint concerning a piece of white plastic found in a packet of crisps, purchased at a supermarket in Coventry. In order to further their investigation, officers visited the Walkers premises in Leicester, where the product was manufactured. During the visit, on the advice of a consultant, the company's Technical Support Manager refused to allow the officers access to parts of the factory that were not connected to the manufacture of the product under investigation. The manager declined to produce records which may have formed part of the company's due diligence defence.

Walkers were convicted on three charges of contravening provisions of the Food Safety Act 1990 by a magistrates' court. The first related to obstruction of officers, in that the Walkers' Technical Support Manager, on the advice of a consultant, failed to give assistance to officers that they reasonably required for performing their functions by denying access to records of control measures at the factory. The second charge for obstruction was similar and related to failure of the manager to allow free access to all relevant parts of the premises. The third charge related to the original food complaint itself and was concerned with the selling of food not of the substance demanded under section 14 of the Act.

The defendant company appealed to the High Court against their conviction, by way of case stated by the Justices. The judgment of the court was given by Rose LJ in answers to six questions put to the court by the Justices. In dismissing the appeal, the court provided some clarification on the powers of authorised officers while investigating possible breaches of food safety legislation. Following this judgment, the Local Authority Coordinating body on Food and Trading Standards (LACORS) issued guidance to food authorities through circular LAC 10 98 2 – *Due Diligence Investigation and the Food Safety Act*. The key conclusions of the judgment are as follows:

- In conducting investigations, authorised officers are entitled to interrogate a possible defence of due diligence, regardless of whether they are exercising their powers within the area of their employing authority or outside it.
- Powers of officers are narrower when they are acting in their 'away team' capacity as they are only entitled to enter business premises and ascertain only whether there 'is' any evidence of contraventions, the emphasis clearly being placed on the present rather than any past breaches.
- While section 33(3) protects a person from answering any question or giving any information which may incriminate him, this does not mean that he can refuse to answer questions or give information in relation to another person or his employer.
- Reliance on expert advice given and received in good faith does not amount to 'reasonable cause' within the meaning of section 33(1)(b) for obstructing an officer in the execution of his duty under the Act.

Powers to inspect, seize and detain records [35]

This is a wide-ranging power to inspect any records, whether they are paper documents or stored on computer. Any such records may be seized or detained if the officer has reason to believe that they may be required as evidence in proceedings. However, the officer is prohibited from disclosing any trade secrets acquired in this way, unless this is unavoidable in the performance of his duty.

Powers to inspect, seize or detain food [36]

Action under section 9 of the Food Safety Act 1990 to inspect, detain and seize food can be taken by an appropriately qualified authorised officer, if it merely appears to him that it fails to meet food safety requirements; no other evidence is necessary. Also, he need not necessarily carry out a physical examination of the food in order to detain or seize it and may be relying on information provided by another food authority or the Food Standards Agency. See p.33 for the application of these powers.

Powers to procure samples [37]

Under section 29, an authorised officer may take a sample of food or any food contact material from any premises without payment, with a view to submitting it for analysis by a public analyst or examination by a food examiner. Details on how samples are to be taken and handled are provided in the Food Safety (Sampling and Qualifications) Regulations 1990 and the Food Safety Act 1990, Code of Practice No. 7 (Revised 2000).

Powers to serve an emergency prohibition notice [38]

Emergency Prohibition Notices may only be signed by a suitably qualified Environmental Health Officer with at least two years, post-qualification experience in food safety matters and who is currently involved in food enforcement duties. [39] See p.34 for further details.

Implications for the food industry

The implementation of emergency powers to deal with food hazards has serious consequences for food businesses, as not only do they face the prospect of losing some or all of their food stocks and possible closure of their premises, they could also be subsequently prosecuted. In some cases, individual food businesses may be the innocent party but are implicated in some way due to their commercial relationship with the primary food business affected by emergency food control measures. If the media is involved, it is quite possible that these secondary businesses may suffer damage to their reputation if the circumstances are such that their activities cannot be distinguished from those of the primary business.

Where, as a result of a Food Hazard Warning, a food business offers to remove the suspect product from sale and surrenders it voluntarily, a signed receipt detailing the description and quantity of food should be obtained from the authorised officer. In the event of a claim being made against an insurance policy for such an incident, the receipt should suffice as proof of lost product. The food business owner should also bear in mind the need for suitable arrangements with respect to the storage, destruction and disposal of the affected food.

Where food is condemned and ordered to be destroyed by a magistrate, the food authority is responsible for arranging its destruction or disposal. Depending on the circumstances, the authorised officer may wish to personally witness the destruction of the food. For small quantities, this may be in a waste compactor; however, if this is not possible at the premises, he may mark it with a conspicuously coloured food dye or disfigure the food in some way to prevent it being brought back into the food supply chain before it is removed from the premises.

Where the emergency arises from a perceived imminent risk of injury from the food premises, the food authority is provided with detailed procedures to follow in the Food Safety Act 1990, Code of Practice No. 6; however, the food business owner's options may be extremely limited. While the law provides for the food business owner to be heard and call witnesses before the magistrates' court (or Sheriff Court), he must act quickly in order to minimise the impact on his business. If the entire premises are subject to closure, while complying with any prohibitions imposed by the Emergency Prohibition Notice and with the authorised officer's consent, it may be possible to minimise further damage to the business. For example, if the emergency action was prompted by the existence of a pest infestation, alternative arrangements could be made for the storage of unaffected food while measures are taken to eliminate the infestation. If the notice only applies to a part of the premises or is limited to a particular machine or process, it may be possible to continue the remaining operation normally, after making appropriate arrangements to satisfy the authorised officer that the prohibitions will not be compromised.

In order to ensure that the prohibitions are lifted as soon as possible, it is imperative that the food business maintains contact with the authorised officer and actively engages in satisfying the officer that there is no longer an imminent risk of injury, notwithstanding the outcome of the court hearing. The food authority must issue a certificate to lift the prohibition within three days of being satisfied that there no longer exists an imminent health risk. The onus is clearly on the food business owner to apply to the food authority to lift the Emergency Prohibition Notice or the Emergency Prohibition Order as soon as possible. On application by the owner, the food authority must determine as soon as is reasonably practicable but within a maximum of 14 days whether or not they are satisfied, and if they are not satisfied, they must give notice of this to the owner with the reasons for their decision. See p.57 on appeals against a food authority's refusal to lift such an order.

As the emergency prohibition procedure provides for the immediate closure of premises or prohibition of a process, there is no advantage to the authorised officer in preferring voluntary action from the food business, although the benefits to the food business are clear. There are numerous reasons for this, including a desire to minimise the impact of formal procedures or detrimental media coverage, or simply to avoid the effects of a copy of the Emergency Prohibition Notice or Emergency Prohibition Order being displayed in a conspicuous position on the premises.

If after considering the circumstances and any risk that the premises may be opened without his knowledge and/or consent the officer agrees to voluntary closure, he is advised to obtain a written undertaking from the proprietor not to reopen without specific permission, although there is no legal sanction against him if he decides to do so. By offering to close voluntarily, however, the proprietor relinquishes his rights to compensation if the court subsequently refuses to make an Emergency Prohibition Order. Also, by surrendering food voluntarily to obviate the need for formal seizure, he foregoes the opportunity to be heard and call witnesses before a JP.

Practical points of interest to food business proprietors
The following points raise important issues and may be of use to food business proprietors subjected to emergency food controls:

- Having taken account of the drawbacks, is it worth offering to surrender food or closing premises voluntarily to avert formal action by the food authority?
- If surrendering food voluntarily, prepare a detailed list of products, including total weight and monetary value.
- If voluntarily surrendered food is to be stored on the premises awaiting destruction, it should be clearly labelled and segregated from unaffected products.
- Do not contravene any conditions required by a Detention of Food Notice.
- Do not contravene any prohibitions imposed by an Emergency Prohibition Notice or Emergency Prohibition Order.
- Do not remove the copy of the Emergency Prohibition Notice or Emergency Prohibition Order from the premises until it ceases to have any effect.
- Devise a plan to minimise the impact of emergency food controls without contravening any prohibitions on the basis of risk assessment. If relevant expertise is not available in-house, serious consideration should be given to appointing a competent food safety consultant. Obtain the agreement of the authorised officer before implementing

any plan to minimise any further damage.

• If food is suspected of failing food safety requirements, consideration should be given to taking samples for independent analysis by an accredited laboratory or food examiner, paying particular attention to any special storage requirements, for example with respect to temperature-sensitive foods.

• If the application for a condemnation order or Emergency Prohibition Order is to be challenged before the magistrate or the court, evidence should be gathered to support your contention, for example photographs, samples, statements from employees.

• Keep detailed records of the events throughout the food emergency incident, including dates, times and witnesses. As soon as possible, obtain written statements from employees, suppliers, contractors or customers that support your contention.

• Inform suppliers or customers promptly if business is likely to be disrupted.

• If you are unsure about any action taken by the authorised officer, do not hesitate to ask for an explanation.

• Without obstructing the authorised officer, take extreme care when offering any information during an investigation into possible breaches of food legislation. It is strongly advised that legal advice is sought as soon as possible and certainly before answering questions under caution.

Defence of due diligence

Under section 21 of the Food Safety Act 1990 and section 22 of the Food and Environment Protection Act 1985, provision is made for a defence. It is a defence for any person charged with an offence under either act to prove that he took all reasonable precautions and exercised all due diligence to avoid the commission of the offence. The burden of proving the defence, on the balance of probability, falls on the defendant.

With respect to prohibitions imposed under the Food and Environment Protection Act 1985, it is a defence for a person charged with an offence to prove that he was acting under instructions from his employer or that he relied in good faith on information supplied to him by another person without any reason to suppose that the information was misleading. In both cases, he must prove that he took all such steps as were reasonably open to him to ensure that no offence would be committed.

Under the Food Safety Act 1990, the due diligence defence is available where the offence relates to a contravention of an Emergency Prohibition Notice,[40] Emergency Prohibition Order[41] or an Emergency Control Order.[42] In practice, the person charged with an offence must prove that all reasonable precautions that could have been taken were taken to avoid the commission of the offence and that all due diligence had been exercised. For example, if the due diligence system includes training of employees as a reasonable precaution, the first task would be to show that the training was suitable for the purpose and secondly that all employees who needed to be trained were in fact trained and that the system included reasonable checks to be carried out by the employer to confirm this.

Under section 21 of the Food Safety Act 1990, a due diligence defence is also available for any person charged with an offence under sections 8, 14 and 15 of the Act, provided they did not prepare the food in question and did not import it into Great Britain. Businesses falling under this category include retailers or wholesalers who may be charged with an offence of selling food not complying with food safety requirements, selling food not of the nature or substance or quality demanded or falsely describing or presenting food. In such cases the requirements of the defence will depend on whether the food is sold as an 'own label' or as a branded product. In both cases, it is a defence to prove that the commission of the offence was due to an act or default of another person who was not under his control, or to reliance on information supplied by such a person. In addition, the person charged must prove that he did not know and had no reason to suspect (or could not reasonably have been expected to know in the case of branded products) at the time of the commission of the alleged offence that his act or omission would amount to an offence. A person selling own-label products is under a further obligation to prove that he carried out reasonable checks or that it was reasonable for him to rely on checks carried out by the person who supplied the food to him.

If the defendant intends to rely on this defence on the basis that the alleged offence was committed due to the act or default of another person, he must serve a notice in writing on the prosecutor at least seven days before the hearing (or within one month of his first appearance in court in connection with the alleged offence). This notice should give details of the other person or the defendant should assist the prosecutor with the identification of that person. If the defendant fails to serve such a notice in advance, he may not rely on this defence unless the court grants him leave to do so.

A prosecution for an offence under the Food Safety Act 1990 may not be begun after three years from the commission of the offence or one year from the discovery by the prosecutor, whichever is the earlier. While food authorities are clearly charged with enforcing the provisions of food safety legislation, it is incumbent on them to ensure that they do not impose requirements on businesses that are over and above those provided for by statute. If the owner of a food business is required by officers of a food authority to undertake unnecessary remedial works beyond those provided for by legal requirements, the authority may be liable to damages. In *Welton (and another)* v. *North Cornwall District Council,*[43] the Court of Appeal dismissed an appeal by the local authority against a judgment of the County Court. Their Lordships held that the local authority was liable for the negligence of an Environmental Health Officer they employed, who had required the plaintiffs, who ran a hotel, to undertake unnecessary remedial works in connection with food hygiene. The court reduced the damages award from £39,522 to £34,000.

Punishment of offences

Under the Food Safety Act 1990, all offences, with the exception of obstruction of authorised officers, are triable in either the magistrates' court or the crown court. A person found guilty of an offence for obstruction is liable on summary conviction (in magistrates' court) to a maximum fine of level 5 on the standard scale or imprisonment for up to three months or both.

For any offence under section 7 (rendering food injurious to health), 8 (selling food not complying with food safety requirements) or 14 (selling food not of the nature or substance or quality demanded) of the 1990 Act, on summary conviction, the fine may be up to £20,000 or imprisonment for up to six months or both. All other offences are punishable by a fine of up to the statutory maximum or imprisonment up to six months or both. However, on conviction on indictment (crown court), the maximum fine is unlimited or imprisonment for up to two years or both.

Any person found guilty of contravening an emergency order under the Food and Environment Protection Act 1985 is liable, on summary conviction, to a fine of up to the statutory maximum, while on conviction on indictment, the fine is unlimited or imprisonment for up to two years or both.

Appeals Against emergency actions

With respect to authorised officers exercising powers to seize food or to impose emergency prohibitions on a business, the decision on whether food meets food safety requirements or if the 'imminent health risk' conditions are met is made by a Justice of the Peace. Where there is clear evidence that a food authority has failed to take into account matters which it ought to have considered and this failure leads to serious consequences, not capable of remedy by the appeal provisions, a judicial review may lie in the High Court. [44]

In dealing with food brought before him, the JP acts in an administrative rather than a judicial capacity. As a result, there is no appeal against his decision to the crown court under section 108 of the Magistrates Court Act 1980. Any person aggrieved by his decision may, however, challenge it by way of judicial review. A number of provisions confer right of appeal against decisions of the enforcing authority and the magistrates' court (Sheriff in Scotland). Any person aggrieved by the decision of an enforcing authority to refuse to issue a certificate lifting an Emergency Prohibition Notice or Emergency Prohibition Order, may appeal to a magistrates' court. [45] This appeal must be made within one month from the food authority's refusal to lift the prohibition. In addition, appeal to the crown court is allowed for any person aggrieved by the decision of a magistrates' court to make a Prohibition Order or an Emergency Prohibition Order. [46] Interestingly, no specific provision is made for a similar appeal against the decision of a Sheriff in Scotland; however, as a result of the judgment and commentary in *East Kilbride District Council v. King,* [47] it is unlikely that Parliament intended to create such an important distinction between England and Scotland. It is possible that such an appeal was considered unnecessary in view of the provisions in sections 27 and 28 of the Sheriff Courts (Scotland) Act 1907. [48]

No such appeal is allowed nor is there any statutory provision made to compensate innocent parties, with respect to an Emergency Control Order (made under section 13 of the Food Safety Act 1990) or an Emergency Order made under the Food and Environment Protection Act 1985, regardless of the circumstances and even if the order is made in error. This is seemingly unfair as situations commonly arise where a food business may be subject to such an order prohibiting certain commercial operation, such as fishing in a designated area or from marketing certain food, where the cause of the hazard is totally out of their control. Under exceptional circumstances, the government may establish compensation schemes, one example of which followed the Chernobyl nuclear incident that caused farmers to suffer considerable losses in their sheep stocks.

In most cases individuals or companies suffering losses must resort to bringing action for damages through the civil courts, provided the organisation responsible can be identified and falls within the jurisdiction of the UK legal system. Although there is no specific provision in the English legal system for a class action to be brought, a large group of individuals who are similarly affected by the failures of a common party may be able to bring collective action under the common law tort of negligence. In *Davies v. Eli Lilly & Co.*[49], the desirability for such actions was expressed by Donaldson MR, stating that courts should be flexible and adaptable in applying existing procedures with a view to reaching a decision quickly and economically, where a large number of plaintiffs are involved. In the majority of cases, however, individuals or organisations would be expected to bring separate actions.

The only option available to any person aggrieved by the making of emergency orders is to seek a judicial review of the Secretary of State's decision. Use was made of this provision by a company whose business was seriously disrupted by the prohibitions imposed by the first ever Emergency Control Order (ECO),[50] where cheese was suspected of being contaminated by *E.coli* 0157. The effect of the order was to prevent the sale or distribution of the suspect cheese, which affected not only the producer of the cheese but also any processors and retailers who were supplied by Duckett & Co. Ltd. One such processor was Eastside Cheese Co., whose business was paralysed by the order. Eastside (together with Ducketts as an interested party) challenged the decision of the Minister to make the order in question through the judicial review process in the High Court.

While dismissing most of the grounds relied on by Eastside, the judge Moses J, in his judgment delivered on 13 November 1998, upheld one ground of challenge and held the ECO to be unlawful. The judge found against the Secretary of State for Health as he had wrongly taken account of considerations of 'administrative convenience' in deciding to make the order. The Secretary of State appealed against this decision to the Court of Appeal.

In the Court of Appeal case *R v. Secretary of State for Health, ex parte Eastside Cheese Co and another,*[51] the Secretary of State relied on the judge's finding that the Department of Health was, under the circumstances, right to regard all cheeses from Ducketts to be unsafe on 19 May, the day before the order was signed. The point of contention was whether the Secretary of State's decision to make the order was correct for reasons of public health and not just to make it easier for the Department of Health to achieve the desired result, that of ensuring that the cheese was taken out of circulation as soon as possible. By demonstrating that the judge had misunderstood what the Department of Health officers had meant by 'testing to destruction' of cheese in the meetings leading up to the order being made, the Secretary of State successfully argued against the judge's decision.

The reasoning behind the Secretary of State's decision to make the order in preference to individual food authorities relying on powers under section 9 of the Food Safety Act 1990 was a technical one. In view of the low infective dose of *E.coli* 0157 – only a small number of organisms are required to cause infection – and the fact that they are not evenly distributed throughout the cheese, it would not be possible to rely on a sampling regime to identify affected batches to guarantee that the organism was absent. While a positive result would clearly indicate contamination, a negative result would only show the absence of the organism in that particular 25 gram sample and could not be relied upon to prove that it was absent from the remaining batch. The only conclusive way to show that the organism was absent from all the cheese would be to test all of it to destruction, which defeats the whole point of the exercise.

Department of Health officials were concerned that reliance on voluntary action from food authorities and the food industry in accordance with the

Food Hazard Warning system may not produce consistent and uniform action quickly enough to warrant the circumstances. Officials were mindful that some food businesses may refuse to surrender the cheese voluntarily, thereby requiring the food authority to formally seize it to bring before a magistrate. The Department of Health envisaged that its resources would not be able to support individual food authorities in proving that the cheese failed to meet food safety requirements. The absence of a reliable sampling regime, together with the inevitable delays resulting from any such sampling in any case, meant that a serious risk to public health would exist. Linked closely to this concern was a perceived reluctance on the part of some food authorities to take action under section 9 for fear of becoming liable for compensation if they failed to convince the magistrate that the cheese was unfit. As a result, Department of Health officials asked the Minister to make the order.

The first order, together with the amended version of the ECO,[52] required food authorities to enforce and execute the prohibition of any commercial operation in relation to cheese originating from Duckett & Co. Ltd. Within their area, however, they were offered protection against any liability to pay compensation if they could not prove that the cheese was unfit. The amendment modified section 9 in such a way that the magistrate only had to be satisfied that the cheese before him fell within the terms of the order and not that it was unfit in order to condemn it. Therefore, the food authority would only be liable in relation to claims for compensation for any damage or deterioration if the cheese brought before the magistrate fell outside the prohibitions imposed by the order.

The Court of Appeal was satisfied that the Secretary of State was right to make the order and that it was not made for the sake of administrative convenience. The court also passed judgment on a number of grounds advanced by Eastside which are of interest, and as this case at the time represented the only such case law on the use of an Emergency Control Order, the findings make for interesting reading. Firstly, Eastside argued that the Minister should have exempted them from the order under the provisions of section 48(1) of the 1990 Act but the judge had not found in the company's favour and the Court of Appeal agreed with his decision. In contrast to his earlier position before the judge, the Secretary of State now agreed that he does indeed have the power to make exemptions by virtue of section 13(3), but Eastside had made no such application.

Even if an application had been made, although there appears to be no particular mechanism laid down under the Act, in view of the Court of Appeal's position it is unlikely that the Secretary of State would have been held to be wrong if he had refused to consent to an exception for Eastside. Clearly the view held by both the judge and the Court of Appeal, envisages section 13 ECOs to be applied uniformly and not selectively. To do so would, in effect, place the exempted companies at an advantage of possibly obtaining compensation from food authorities if JPs find in their favour following seizure of food under section 9. Other significant points of this judgment were that the Secretary of State was held not to have breached the principle of *proportionality* in making the order. This is a key tenet of European Community law and requires that the disadvantages caused by the effects of any law must not be disproportionate to the aims pursued.

While Article 34 (of the EC Treaty), which prohibits any measures which restrict trade between Member States, had clearly been breached by the making of the order, this was justified under Article 36, which does not preclude 'prohibitions...justified on grounds of...protection of health and life of humans...'. Curiously, the Court of Appeal permitted an argument to be advanced which had not been raised in the High Court before the judge, whereby Eastside contended that the Secretary of State could not rely on Article 36, as their fundamental human rights under Article 1 of Protocol 1 of the European Convention on Human Rights had been violated. It is probable that the court was mindful that the principles of this provision, to which the UK government was a signatory, were to be brought into force in this country through the Human Rights Act 1998, from October 2000. Article 1 of Protocol 1 provides that:

Every natural or legal person is entitled to the peaceful enjoyment of his possessions. No one shall be deprived of his possessions except in the public interest and subject to the conditions provided for by law and by the general principles of international law.

The preceding provisions shall not, however, in any way impair the right of a State to enforce such laws as it deems necessary to control the use of property in accordance with the general interest or to secure the payment of taxes or other contributions or penalties.

On this point, the Court of Appeal held that the action taken by the Secretary of State did not violate the fundamental human rights on the part of Ducketts and Eastside. The Secretary of State's appeal was, therefore, allowed.

Notes

1. JFSSG (1999b) Planning the FSA Response to a Major Food Emergency, CP(99)38/3.
2. Section 9(3)(b), Food Safety Act 1990.
3. Food Safety Act 1990, Code of Practice No. 4 – Inspection, Detention and Seizure of Suspect Food.
4. Section 9(5)(a), Food Safety Act 1990.
5. Section 9(6)(a), Food Safety Act 1990.
6. Section 9(6)(b), Food Safety Act 1990.
7. Section 9(4), Food Safety Act 1990.
8. Section 9(7), Food Safety Act 1990.
9. Section 12(1), Food Safety Act 1990.
10. Section 12(7), Food Safety Act 1990.
11. Section 12(3), Food Safety Act 1990.
12. Section 12(2), Food Safety Act 1990.
13. Section 12(8), Food Safety Act 1990.
14. Enforcement of the Food Safety Act 1990 in relation to the Food Hazard Warning System (HMSO, 1997).
15. T.H. Pennington (1997) Report on the circumstances leading to the 1996 outbreak of infection with E.Coli 0157 in Central Scotland, the implications for food safety and the lessons to be learned (Stationery Office).
16. Section 40(2)(a), Food Safety Act 1990.
17. Section 40(2)(b), Food Safety Act 1990.
18. Food (Cheese) (Emergency Control) Order 1998 (SI 1998/1277).
19. Pennington (1997). See 15 above
20. Section 13(1), Food Safety Act 1990.
21. Section 13(3), Food Safety Act 1990.
22. SI 1998/1277.
23. The Food (Peanuts from Egypt) (Emergency Control) (England and Wales) Order 2000 (SI 2000/375).
24. Section 1(1), Food and Environment Protection Act 1985.
25. Food Protection (Emergency Prohibitions) (Radioactivity in Sheep) Order 1991 (SI 1991/20).
26. Food Protection (Emergency Prohibitions) (Paralytic Shellfish Poisoning) Order 1994 (SI 1994/2029).
27. Section 2, Food and Environment Protection Act 1985.
28. Errington v. Wilson [1995] SLT 1193.
29. Report by Sheriff J. Douglas Allan (1995) Sheriff's Decision on the Application under section 9 of the Food Safety Act 1990 by Clydesdale District Council (Sheriffdom of South Strathclyde, Dumfries and Galloway at Lanark).
30. J.P. Summers (1997) 'Listeria Monocytogenes in Cheese – Implications for Food safety Enforcement' (REHIS, unpublished).
31. www.alma-services.co.uk/cannon/lanarkblue/lanarkblue_009.html.
32. Section 32, Food Safety Act 1990.
33. Section 33, Food Safety Act 1990.
34. [1998] 3 All ER 163.
35. Section 32(6), Food Safety Act 1990.
36. Section 9, Food Safety Act 1990.

37. Section 29, Food Safety Act 1990.
38. Section 12, Food Safety Act 1990.
39. Food Safety Act 1990, Code of Practice No. 6 – Prohibition Procedures (HMSO).
40. Section 12, Food Safety Act 1990.
41. Ibid.
42. Section 13, Food Safety Act 1990.
43. [1977] 1 WLR.
44. See Associated Picture Houses Ltd v. Wednesbury Corporation [1947] 2 All ER 680.
45. Section 37, Food Safety Act 1990.
46. Section 38, Food Safety Act 1990.
47. [1996] SLT 30.
48. K. Thompson (1997) 'Right of Apeal under the Food Safety Act 1990' Juridical Review, 254.
49. [1987] 3 All ER 94.
50. Food (Cheese) (Emergency Control) Order 1998 (SI 1998/1277).
51. [1999] 3 CMLR 123.
52. SI 1998/1284.

Chapter 5
Prevention of food emergencies

Food emergencies invariably involve some form of contamination or change to food resulting in undesirable consequences to humans. Emergencies may arise from food being contaminated by a wide range of undesirable contaminants; however, these can be placed into one or more of the following categories, namely biological, physical and chemical contamination.

Although the cause of food emergencies may vary enormously, the focus of this book is on the more probable causes that arise during food production, processing, distribution and retailing. However, the key preventative and control principles discussed in this chapter may well be applicable to other types of emergency. Clearly, in the interest of ensuring consumer safety as the primary aim, the food industry should implement effective systems to prevent food hazards arising from biological, physical or chemical contamination in the first place. Where the food hazard only manifests itself at the post-production stage, systems for crisis management to remove the suspect food from the food supply chain are discussed in Chapter 6.

In order to ensure that consumers are provided with safe food, it is necessary to consider all possible sources of contamination throughout the process from primary production on the farm through to consumption in the home or a commercial outlet. In view of a number of high-profile cases, where food has been used to extort or blackmail food businesses, the possibility of deliberate acts of adulteration or contamination must be considered alongside accidental contamination at all stages. However, it may be more probematic to take precautions against a determined person with access to the food during production or processing, such as a disgruntled employee.

In a case that has become infamous due to food contamination being used to blackmail food companies, Rodney Francis Witchelo,[1] a former Detective Sergeant in the Metropolitan Police was imprisoned for 17 years in December 1990. Witchelo was convicted of six offences of blackmail, two of contaminating goods with intent to cause economic loss, one of threatening to kill and two of attempting to obtain by deception. During a trial lasting 44 days, the court heard that Witchelo had meticulously planned and executed an elaborate scheme to blackmail two food companies, namely Heinz and Pedigree Petfoods. In addition to threats made in writing, he contaminated food on numerous occasions and placed it on the shelves of stores for the public to purchase. The contamination included mercury, caustic soda, drawing pins and razor blades. Out of sheer good fortune no consumers were injured, although on one occasion, a small piece of razor had to be retrieved from a baby's mouth by a mother who had purchased a jar of contaminated baby food.

In return for stopping this long campaign of terror, Witchelo demanded large sums up to £400,000 from the companies to be paid into building society accounts opened under false names so that he could extract the money through the Link network of cash dispensing machines across the country. He successfully managed to obtain £32,000 but was eventually arrested outside a building society after a massive police operation to trace him. Witchelo's appeal against the sentence to the Court of Appeal was dismissed, as the sentence was not considered to be excessive in view of the seriousness of the offences.

Law Dealing with food contamination

Legislation dealing with food contamination can be divided into two types, namely those provisions which prohibit contamination in the first place and those which make it an offence for any person to sell, offer, expose or advertise for sale such food. Firstly, there are regulations,[2] which require all food, which is handled, stored, packaged, displayed and transported to be protected:

> ... against any contamination likely to render the food unfit for human consumption, injurious to health or contaminated in such a way that it would be unreasonable to expect it to be consumed in that state.

Section 7 of the Food Safety Act 1990, which can be traced back to the Public Health Act 1872, makes it an offence for any person to render food injurious to health by the addition of a harmful article or substance, among other operations. Importantly, however, this offence requires proof that the food was intended to be sold for human consumption. This reflects the possibility of deliberate contamination of food by adulteration, reminiscent of the nineteenth century and not used very often today. However, this provision could be applicable if food is rendered injurious to health by the addition of pesticides or the use of antibiotics and growth hormones in food animals. Since September 11 and the increased likelihood of food terrorism, this section could be equally applicable to offences related to the deliberate contamination of food intended for human consumption with harmful substances.

The wide-ranging nature of provisions in the Food Safety Act 1990 are well suited to modern offences concerning contamination. Section 8 of this Act makes it an offence for any person to sell, offer, expose or advertise food that fails to meet food safety requirements. Food fails to meet food safety requirements if:

(a) it has been rendered injurious to health by means of any of the operations mentioned in section 7(1);
(b) it is unfit for human consumption; or
(c) it is so contaminated that it would be unreasonable to expect it to be used for human consumption in that state.[3]

Where food has been contaminated by foreign bodies such as glass, metals and plastics, etc. or by mould or where the quality of the food has deteriorated, it may be easier to use section 14 of the Act. Under section 14(1):

any person who sells to the purchaser's prejudice any food which is not of the nature, substance or quality demanded by the consumer is guilty of an offence.

Preventative and protective measures against food contamination

In order to minimise the risk of food emergencies arising in the first place, the food industry has developed many systems to suit particular circumstances over the years. For many years food manufacturers and processors relied on quality control techniques to evaluate the safety of the final product but often this was based on end product inspection and testing, where a sampling plan was devised to analyse a small proportion of each batch of production for defects. However, this approach could not be relied upon to detect all the potential hazards as the emphasis was placed on the end product and, in some cases, results of microbiological or compositional analysis would only become available once the product had been despatched to the retailer for sale.

Even if results were available, a random sampling regime representing a small proportion of production could not be relied upon to detect contamination which was not homogeneously distributed throughout the food, for example microbiological contamination, without carrying out destructive testing of 100 per cent of the batch thereby defeating the purpose. To address the shortcomings of quality control as a technique, a different approach was needed, one that enabled any potential problems within food production to be predicted in advance, so that corrective action could be taken before the product was released from the manufacturing plant with the potential of exposing the consumer to a risk of illness or injury. One such technique is Hazard Analysis and Critical Control Point (HACCP), as described below.

Hazard Analysis and Critical Control Point (HACCP)

Against the background of uncertainty about the safety of food, a new approach to ensuring a 'nil defects' system of food production was sought by the National Aeronautics and Space Administration (NASA), as a part of the United States Space Programme in the late 1960s. Working in conjunction with NASA and the United States Army Laboratory, the Pillsbury Company developed a new food safety management system based on the engineering system of Failure Mode and Effects Analysis (FMEA). The principles of (HACCP) were developed further and formally adopted by the Codex Alimentarius Commission as a system for achieving a consistency of approach in ensuring food safety throughout Member Countries of the United Nations.

As a system, HACCP has many strengths but the focus is clearly on food safety and it can be applied to any process from primary production, manufacturing, processing, distribution and retail through to final consumption. Also, it can be applied readily to all types of food production from large-scale production units to a small delicatessen. Importantly, HACCP relies on the application of quality assurance techniques throughout the whole process rather than concentrating on inspection and testing of the end product. It is based on a proactive approach to firstly identify where hazards may occur within a process and then taking the necessary action to prevent those hazards being realised. In this way, many potential hazards may be designed out of the process, while others will be prevented or minimised to acceptable levels.

By identifying the 'critical control points' (CCP) for a process, this technique will enable valuable resources such as money, time and manpower to be concentrated on the most important control measures to ensure that the final product is safe each time. As the system is logical and based on risk assessment to establish whether a hazard exists and the controls necessary to prevent the hazard, it allows a pragmatic approach to be applied to managing food safety, rather than the traditional prescriptive approach. The following example demonstrates the technique involved in applying HACCP principles to a simple process.

Example

To illustrate the usefulness of HACCP as a technique, let us consider a straightforward bakery process, where the basic ingredients of flour, water and yeast are mixed into a dough, shaped and baked in an oven to make loaves of bread. For this example, a simple hazard analysis process identifies a hazard to the consumer from physical contamination such as metal. The source of this metal may vary, including raw materials, machinery, the premises and the baking tin itself; however, a number of controls may be employed to eliminate or reduce to acceptable limits the possibility that metal may be present in the final product. These include sieving flour, cleaning of plant and machinery, maintenance procedures for machinery and metal detection. Indeed, metal detectors may be present at numerous points throughout the process, including one at the very end, where the packaged loaf of bread passes through a metal detector before being despatched to customers. If metal in excess of the set specifications for the machine, for example, 1 mm, is detected, the machine will sound an alarm and stop the conveyor belt or automatically reject the suspect food into a locked container.

Clearly, all control measures for preventing metal contamination are important; however, by applying the principles of HACCP, it is possible to identify one particular point that is critical to food safety, in other words the Critical Control Point (CCP). This may be described as the last point in the process at which control may be exercised to prevent a food hazard and failure at this point will pose a risk to food safety.

With respect to the example, the critical control point for metal contamination of bread is the last metal detector, as this will reject any product that contains metal, regardless of the source and the stage in the process where metal contamination took place. While the other metal detectors may be important in minimising damage to machinery from the presence of metal in the product, they are not critical to food safety as any failures that allow metal contamination should always be detected by the last detector and the product rejected.

This system will enable the factory management confidently to prioritise control procedures in such a way as to concentrate on the effective operation of the last metal detector, including maintenance, calibration and regular testing using a standard 1 mm test piece. While not ignoring other control measures, this system enables valuable resources to be focused on the most important controls within the process to ensure food safety from the risk of metal contamination, every time.

The Codex Alimentarius Commission has published a revised version of the HACCP system together with guidelines for its application.[4] In order to enhance understanding of the seven principles of HACCP, the Commission has also published the following definitions:[5]

Control (verb): To take all necessary actions to secure and maintain compliance with criteria established in the HACCP plan.

Control (noun): The state wherein correct procedures are being followed and criteria are being met.

Control measure: Any action and activity that can be used to prevent or eliminate a food safety hazard or reduce it to an acceptable level.

Critical Control Point (CCP): A step at which control can be applied and is essential to prevent or eliminate a food safety hazard or reduce it to an acceptable level.

Critical limit: A criterion which separates acceptability from unacceptability.

Deviation: Failure to meet a critical limit.

Flow diagram: A systematic representation of the sequence of steps or operations used in the production or manufacture of a particular food item.

HACCP: A system which identifies, evaluates, and controls hazards which are significant for food safety.

HACCP plan: A document prepared in accordance with the principles of HACCP to ensure control of hazards which are significant for food safety in the segment of the food chain under consideration.

Hazard: A biological, chemical or physical agent in, or condition of, food with the potential to cause an adverse health effect.

Hazard analysis: The process of collecting and evaluating information on hazards and conditions leading to their presence to decide which are significant for food safety and therefore should be addressed in the HACCP plan.

Monitor: The act of conducting a planned sequence of observations or measurements of control parameters to assess whether a CCP is under control.

Step: A point, procedure, operation or stage in the food chain including raw materials, from primary production to final consumption.

Validation: Obtaining evidence that the elements of the HACCP plan are effective.

Verification: The application of methods, procedures, tests and other evaluation, in addition to monitoring to determine compliance with the HACCP plan.

Seven principles of HACCP [6]

Principle 1 – Conduct a hazard analysis
Starting with a breakdown of the food process into a series of logical steps where hazards may occur, a flow diagram is compiled by a multidisciplinary HACCP team. This should include all stages, from receiving raw materials through to the final product. When this is complete, the HACCP team identify all the hazards, whether biological, chemical or physical, which could occur at each stage and next to each one describe the control measures needed to prevent the hazard from being realised.

Principle 2 – Determine the critical control points (CCPs)
When all the hazards and control measures have been listed, the CCP's should be identified, possibly with the use of a decision tree. These are points where control is critical to ensuring food safety.

Principle 3 – Establish critical limit(s)
A critical limit is defined above but it should be a parameter capable of being measured, for example temperature or time. Sometimes the critical limit will simply be the absence of a particular condition, for example absence of foreign bodies.

Principle 4 – Establish a system to monitor control of the CCP
Once critical limits have been established for each CCP, the method of monitoring the parameters is developed. In addition, the frequency of monitoring and the person responsible for implementing it is decided.

Principle 5 – Establish the corrective action to be taken when monitoring indicates that a particular CCP is not under control
This step specifies exactly what action is to be taken in the event of a deviation from the critical limit to bring the process under control and by whom, so that all those charged with the responsibility of operating the HACCP system are left in no doubt.

Principle 6 – Establish procedures for verification to confirm that the HACCP system is working effectively
This may be done as a part of a wider quality management system or as stand-alone procedures by the HACCP team. Inevitably, this will require a

system for recording the fact that the system is operating within parameters of the process controls, whether on computer or by means of written documents.

Principle 7 – Establish documentation concerning all procedures and records appropriate to these principles and their application
Suitable records must be kept to demonstrate that the HACCP system is working correctly to guarantee food safety.

In 1993, the Codex Alimentarius Commission recommended that national governments should incorporate HACCP principles into their legislation. These were adopted by the European Union through Council Directive 93/43/EEC[7] and subsequently implemented in the UK through Regulation 4(3) of the Food Safety (General Food Hygiene) Regulations 1995,[8] albiet in a somewhat diluted form. However, since then, the full HACCP principles have been enshrined into UK legislation fully on a number of occasions, for example through the Food Safety (General Food Hygiene) (Butchers' Shops) Amendment Regulations 2000.[9]

Advantages of HACCP

There are a number of advantages of the HACCP system, not only in ensuring safe food but also in improving quality and cost-effectiveness, that are worthy of mention:

- If the monitoring of CCPs shows a deviation from the specification, for example the minimum cooking temperature of food, the remedial action can be taken during processing rather than waiting until test results are available, at which point it may be too late to act leading to product wastage.

- As parameters such as time, temperature or pH, are easy to monitor, operators are not left in any doubts as to the necessity for corrective action.
- Concentrating scarce resources in areas of greatest need promotes cost-effective control measures.

- The system relies on the involvement of all staff which, if properly managed, will lead to team working and improved morale.

• There is a reduction in product wastage and savings can be made from avoiding the reprocessing of the product.

• HACCP complements other quality management systems based on ISO 9001 and good manufacturing practices.

• The documentation generated during the process will be useful in demonstrating compliance with legislation, such as Regulation 4(3) of the Food Safety (General Food Hygiene) Regulations 1995 or as part of a 'due diligence' statutory defence under section 21 of the Food Safety Act 1990. In addition, documentation will be extremely useful in quickly identifying and isolating suspect batches of food in the event of a product withdrawal or recall.

Clearly, the HACCP system is extremely thorough and has been proven to be effective over many decades throughout the world, not only in producing safe food with a high degree of confidence but also in ensuring that it remains safe during subsequent stages until it reaches the final consumer. Like any other management system, however, HACCP has its limitations and it is only as good as the competence and commitment of the people who established it in the first place and those responsible for maintaining it. In considering techniques for preventing and controlling food emergencies, the managers of a food business must be prepared for all potential hazards that could present a risk of injury to consumers. By continuing the proactive approach of the HACCP system, it is possible to predict possible food safety hazards that may arise once the product has been despatched to the subsequent stages of the food supply chain until it reaches the final customer.

However, even if the HACCP system works perfectly, it is possible that the product may be subjected to a subsequent process which makes it unsafe or the food hazard may only become apparent at some later stage. In some cases the safety of food may be compromised due to failures in the systems operated by suppliers. However, the rapid control of such a situation may depend on the effectiveness of food safety management systems of businesses further along the food supply chain such as processors, manufacturers or retailers. It is for this reason that prudent managers should include in their food safety management system suitable arrangements for dealing with emergencies, whether as a stand-alone system or as part of wider crisis management procedures. The key to the success of any such system, however, is effective planning.

Mechanisms for controlling food emergencies

In order for any food business to minimise the impact of a food emergency on consumers and the continuity of their business, it is absolutely critical for the suspect batch or consignment of food to be identified quickly and accurately, followed by its efficient removal from the food supply chain, as time is truly of the essence. For this to be achieved, suitable mechanisms must be in place to identify and trace food throughout the food supply chain. Where food is made up from numerous raw ingredients, traceability must be achieved from the final product backwards through any stages of production to its constituent ingredients. Incidentally, it is worth noting that traceability principles must extend to any food packaging materials used, as these may be a source of contamination.

Failure to take swift action could be disastrous for the food business. Imagine a scenario where a food manufacturer is implicated in a 'food scare' and their product is suspected of posing a serious food safety risk. Regardless of the truthfulness of the allegation against the company, if the suspect food can be quickly identified and isolated to known production batches, the sophisticated distribution systems of the major food manufacturers or retailers can ensure the rapid removal of food from the food chain, pending further analysis or investigation. This type of situation may be managed relatively easily without causing serious disruption to the day-to-day operations of the company.

Conversely, if the inadequacy or absence of traceability means that the suspect batch cannot be identified accurately, the company may have no option but to stop production and recall potentially huge quantities of product which may already be in circulation, despite the fact that it is perfectly safe and fit for human consumption. This may result in large quantities of recalled stock being quarantined or destroyed, while leaving the company unable to continue operations until new supplies can be sourced from acceptable suppliers.

If the suspect food is subject to a formal investigation by a food authority, section 8(3) of the Food Safety Act 1990 provides:

> ...where any food which fails to comply with food safety requirements is part of a batch, lot or consignment of food of the same class or description, it shall be presumed for the purposes of this section and section 9, below until the contrary is proved, that all of the food in that batch, lot or consignment fails to comply with those requirements

Consequently, unless a food manufacturer, for instance, was able to prove otherwise, say by means of a suitable documented traceability system, an authorised officer may require the whole batch, lot or consignment to be detained, pending further investigation or to seize it in order to have it dealt with by a Justice of the Peace (see Chapter 4, p.33).

Traceability

Traceability is defined as:

> ... the ability to trace and follow a food, feed, food-producing animal or substance intended to be, or expected to be incorporated into a food or feed, through all stages of production, processing and distribution.[10]

There is no single prescribed method for enabling traceability of food; however, the food industry has developed a variety of coding systems that allow the final product to be traced back to its source and constituent ingredients or materials. Provided the integrity of the traceability system can be demonstrated to be intact, the particular mechanisms employed for achieving this are not of crucial importance.

One such method is to incorporate a Julian calendar code indicating the day and year of production, as well as further information such as the time, shift or production line number, on the final product labelling. Another way of enabling traceability to the day of production is to make use of the durability code that may be required to be displayed on the product under food labelling requirements, such as the 'Use by' or 'Best before' date. As the product is allocated a known shelf life, a simple calculation should reveal the day of production.

Once the day and time of production is known from the coding on the final product, the production or process records for that day or production run should provide details of which batch of individual ingredients were used to make up the final product. In turn, stock control records should identify the particular supplier, date of receiving the product, durability codes (if relevant), temperature (if relevant) and condition of the product, for each ingredient.

In the event that a manufacturer is notified of a suspect batch of raw materials by the supplier or another source, the traceability system should also work in reverse, to enable all final products made from the suspect batch of raw materials to be readily identified and, if appropriate, recalled if they are already in circulation.

Understandably, some companies may wish to utilise a unique coding system known only to them in order to protect commercially sensitive information. Developments in new technology have opened up endless possibilities for enabling traceability of food by means of sophisticated and operationally efficient bar coding or tagging systems, enabling the business not only to trace products throughout the process but also to exercise strict controls over purchasing requirements, work in progress and production outputs.

Law concerning traceability [11]

Although there is currently no general duty on food businesses to establish product traceability systems, there are a number of exceptions in special circumstances. These are as follows:

• From 1 September 2000, the Compulsory Beef Labelling Scheme (CBLS) enables the slaughterhouse and cutting plants for fresh and frozen beef to be identified at the point of sale.

• The British Cattle Movement Service (an agency of the Department for the Environment, Food and Rural Affairs (DEFRA)) runs a mandatory identification and registration scheme in the UK. This requires all cattle to be registered with the agency and for all movements of the animals born after 1 January 1998 to be traced.

• Premises where food of animal origin (meat, meat products, minced meat and meat preparations, wild-game meat, milk and milk products, egg products, fish and shellfish) is handled or processed are subject to more stringent hygiene controls under UK regulations made to implement European 'vertical' directives. Consignments of such foods are required to carry a health mark denoting the approval number of the premises issued by the relevant competent authority, allowing some traceability;

• The provisions of the General Product Safety Regulations 1994,[12] place a general duty on a 'producer' of food to adopt measures to enable him to be informed of the risk that his product presents and to take appropriate action, including marking the product or batches of product and withdrawing the product from circulation. It is worth noting, however, that in practice, these regulations are likely to be enforced by Trading Standards Officers, while the authorised officers who enforce food safety legislation are usually Environmental Health Officers. While the structure of local authorities means that the Trading Standards and Environmental Health function is likely to be within the same department (except where the county council still has responsibility for trading standards), this is an area where considerable coordinated effort would be required to achieve the desired outcome. Although the regulations are aimed primarily at manufacturers, the term producer may, in some circumstances, include retailers, for example, where the retailer sells 'own label' products or imports products.

• Although the Food Labelling Regulations 1996 and the Food (Lot Marking) Regulations 1996 require certain foods to be labelled with descriptions including durability codes and lot marking, there are foods to which these regulations do not apply, such as open food sold directly to the ultimate consumer.

• The Feeding Stuffs Regulations 2000 require labelling of feed material and enable some traceability, as do the Materials in Contact with Food Regulations 1987 with respect to packaging materials used for food.

• The Food Irradiation Provisions (England) Regulations 2000 require irradiated food to be suitably labelled to indicate this fact and identify the premises where the processing took place.

Most large food manufacturers are likely to incorporate traceability and product recall procedures as part of accredited quality management systems such as ISO 9001.[13] For 'own label' foods produced on behalf of large multiple retailers, the British Retail Consortium (BRC) Technical Standard for Own Label Foods also requires effective traceability systems to be in place. However, as the most serious food poisoning outbreak in the UK (*E.coli* 0157 in Lanarkshire) originated from a butcher's shop, these limited voluntary arrangements were of little use.

In any food emergency, one of the most critical factors in minimising the risks to the consumer is to quickly identify the cause of the food hazard and to evaluate the extent or scale of the hazard so that appropriate action can be taken to isolate and remove from circulation the affected batch or consignment. In the absence of a general legal requirement to establish systems to trace a product to its constituent parts at present and to maintain sufficient records of the destination of the finished product, it is conceivable that the best intentions of the food business and regulatory authorities may be frustrated by the inadequacy of suitable records. Failure to keep such records by businesses could be extremely damaging in the event of a food emergency requiring a product recall, as food authorities acting in the public interest may be forced to detain or seize whole batches or consignments of food unnecessarily, purely as a precaution. In the General Food Law Regulation,[14] a requirement for traceability of food, feed, food-producing animal and any other substance intended to be or expected to be incorporated into food or feed has been introduced by Article 18 (see Chapter 8, p.121).

Scotland takes a stance on traceability

In a unilateral move to reflect the strength of concern over food safety from butchers' shops in response to the *E.coli* 0157 food poisoning outbreak in Lanarkshire, regulations requiring butchers' premises to be licensed[15] in Scotland place additional duties on proprietors with respect to product recall. In contrast to the equivalent regulations in England, those in Scotland require the proprietor (or his delegated representative) of each butcher's shop supplying to other commercial operations or to large 'event deliveries', such as parties and weddings, to maintain accurate records of the description, quantity, date of production, date of delivery and delivery address, to enable an effective product recall to be conducted in the event of a food emergency. Additionally, in relation to food sold at retail level, the licence holder is required, at his own expense, to ensure adequate publicity to alert customers to the risk to their safety and inform them of the recall procedure, as well as keeping the relevant licensing authority advised of the product recall.

This is certainly useful in enabling suspect food to be traced in one direction from the butcher to known destinations. However, there are no requirements for individual batches to be labelled with its source. With respect to meat in particular, once it has been prepared into small portions or minced, it is almost impossible to distinguish one batch from another. If a hazard was identified after preparation, it will not be possible to trace it to its source unless the business carrying out the processing operates an effective independent traceability system of their own.

Notes

1. R v. Witchelo [1992] 13 Cr App R (S) 371.
2. Regulation 4(2)(d), Food Safety (General Food Hygiene) Regulations 1995 (Chapter IX).
3. Section 8(2), Food Safety Act 1990.
4. Codex Alimentarius Commission (1997) Food Hygiene Basic Texts – HACCP System and Guidelines for Its Application, Annex to CAC/RCP 1 – 1969, Rev. 3 (Rome: FAO).
5. Reproduced with the kind permission of the Food and Agriculture Organisation of the United Nations.
6. Codex Alimentarius Commission (1997).
7. Of 14 June 1993 on the Hygiene of Foodstuffs, OJ L175, 19.7.93, p. 1.
8. SI 1995/1763.
9. SI 2000/930.
10. Article 3, EU General Food Law Regulation, 178/2002, OJ L31/1, 1.2.2002.
11. Food Standards Agency (2002) Traceability in the Food Chain - A Preliminary Study.
12. Regulation 8(b).
13. BS EN ISO 9001: 2000 (International Organisation for Standards).
14. EC 178/2002, OJ L31/1, 1.2.2002.
15. Food Safety (General Food Hygiene) (Butchers' Shops) Amendment (Scotland) Regulations 2000.

Chapter 6
Control of food emergencies

If a food emergency arises despite preventative measures as discussed in the previous chapter, it must be brought under control as quickly as possible. As every minute that passes increases the risk of harm to the consumer, there will be no time to waste. An emergency is not the time to test out procedures for the first time. A tried and tested crisis management system is therefore vital.

Crisis Management

In formulating their crisis management plan a food business must take account of all possible scenarios concerning their product. They are expert in producing their product but the cause of the crisis may vary. Mundane events can range from power failures during production, breakdowns in chilled or frozen storage to the possibility of fuel shortages that affect distribution. For the purpose of this work, it is the crises which result from food emergencies that will be discussed in detail from hereon. Bland defines a crisis as follows:

> A serious incidence affecting, for example, human safety, the environment, and/or product or corporate reputation and which has either received or been threatened by adverse publicity.[1]

From the case studies discussed earlier, it is clear that companies that manage to achieve the dual goal of protecting the consumer while at the same time maintaining their commercial integrity are those which have implemented a predetermined and well-rehearsed plan.

Although there is no legal requirement on the food industry to prepare a crisis management system with respect to food, there is an overwhelming case for businesses to develop systems to deal with food emergencies, not only for safeguarding consumer safety but for protecting their brands. In some cases, where the product poses no risk to consumer safety but falls short of the company's normal standards, for example in quality or packaging, it may be appropriate to withdraw the product from the market and return it once corrective measures are taken. This is not uncommon in the food industry and products are withdrawn from the trade, the so called 'silent withdrawal', without much disruption to the day-to-day operations of the company concerned.

Before progressing further to consider how a company may bring a food emergency under control, it is useful to examine the most probable causes of hazards. These include the following:

- a defect in the composition of food itself, including ingredients or its packaging;
- a manufacturing or processing error;
- biological, physical or chemical contamination;
- incorrect or inaccurate information on the product or accompanying the product; and
- malicious product tampering or extortion.

Product recall

In the vast majority of cases, a crisis may be effectively managed and brought under control without the need to recall the product. However, should it be necessary, the business should be in a position to implement a predetermined recall plan. While the particular circumstances of the hazard will dictate the exact response, the options available to companies will vary widely from doing nothing through to instigating a full-scale product recall.

According to the joint Australia New Zealand Food Authority (ANZFA) the definition of a recall is:

> action taken to remove from sale, distribution and consumption, foods which pose a safety hazard to consumers.[2]

In order to satisfy the objective of protecting consumers by quickly and efficiently removing suspect food from the supply chain, the recall plan must be sufficiently comprehensive to deal effectively with every likely eventuality and unambiguous in terms of the aim to be achieved. It should also outline the responsibilities of all personnel involved, the procedures to be implemented and the basis of decision-making.

Is a product recall necessary?

The plan should include the mechanism for intelligence-gathering and the criteria to be used to enable decision-making, from the initial decision to implement a recall through to the post-recall assessment in order to establish the effectiveness of the whole exercise. The decision to implement a recall in the first place must be formalised and should be based on a set of criteria to be determined by senior management. The factors to be considered may vary from one business to the next depending on the approach to risk management but, as the Perrier case demonstrated, food safety is not the only reason for a recall. In addition to the obvious reason of safeguarding consumers, companies will place great importance on protecting their brand name. This alone may warrant a product recall.

The effectiveness of any crisis management system relies on the availability of accurate and reliable information, so particular emphasis should be placed on the intelligence-gathering mechanisms. Early warning systems should be in place for detecting and rapidly reporting any potential recall situations to senior management. The quicker the recall team becomes aware of a potential problem, the quicker the appropriate response can be instigated. Sources of information on a product complaint and a potential product recall situation include:

- internal monitoring procedures;
- customers;
- suppliers;
- local food authority or home authority;
- Food Standards Agency;
- general practitioner (GP), hospital or health authority;
- media.

Food complaint handling system

While the source of information may vary, it is imperative for all such alerts to be directed to a central food complaint handling system. This is particularly relevant for companies with multiple operating units throughout the country or even abroad, so that information is available as soon as possible to the person who is charged with the responsibility for deciding whether the complaint is dealt with through the normal food complaint handling procedure or forwarded to the recall coordinator.

Personnel involved with receiving food complaints should be trained to ensure that the following details are collected:

- complainant's personal details: name, address, contact telephone number(s);
- reason for complaint;
- details of suspect product: product name, size, durability codes, markings, is a sample available?
- time, date and place where suspect product was purchased;
- how was the suspect product transported after purchase (if relevant)?
- where and how was product stored after purchase?
- how was the suspect product handled, prepared or cooked (if relevant)?
- time, date and place where complaint was discovered;
- details of alleged injury or illness:
– time and date of consumption of product;
– whether product consumed previously;
– number of persons consuming product;
– number of persons suffering illness or injury;
– details of persons affected: names, contact details, age, symptoms in each case;
– details of any treatment administered by a medical practitioner and contact details for GP surgery or hospital.

A majority of product complaints will be processed through the food complaint handling procedure and this should include an accurate record of the action taken in response to each case. In very exceptional cases, the pre-determined criteria for a product recall may be satisfied and the recall coordinator should be informed of a potential product recall situation.

Recall plan

In order for the suspect product to be removed from the food supply chain quickly and efficiently, a series of steps is suggested in the next section on p.92 but the success of the recall plan will depend on a number of key prerequisites being in place.

Endorsement by the executive management

The recall plan must have the full support and endorsement of management, together with the allocation of necessary resources.

Who will be the recall coordinator?

This is a crucial role as the recall coordinator is responsible for leading the activities of the recall team and must have a good all-round knowledge of the key functions of the business. Usually the role is fulfilled by the head of the technical function but clearly will involve close liaison with the managing director or equivalent, as the person with the authority to make the final decision.

Who will be on the recall team?

The recall team should comprise the heads of each key function within the company, including production, sales, marketing, quality, technical, legal, warehousing and distribution. It is common for the person with the authority to make the final decision on action taken to be included on the team but this is not always the case, provided the line of responsibility for decision-making is clear. Deputies should be appointed for each member in the event that they are not available for any reason. Job descriptions should identify the roles for each member and accurate 24-hour contact details should be maintained and reviewed for accuracy at three-monthly intervals.

In order to ensure a clear and consistent message is presented to those outside the organisation, all communications should flow through a single channel. The ultimate responsibility for communicating with external agencies and the media should be assigned to a single person with experience in this field, and preferably training in public relations. Alternatively, the services of a reputable public relations company should be retained to provide expertise in this critical area. In all cases, the outgoing message from the food company should closely follow the Risk Communication Strategy developed in advance during the planning stage.

For smaller businesses, the arrangements should reflect the size and nature of the operation. If the entire workforce consists of a small number of staff, it may be appropriate for the recall to be managed by just one person with assistance from other staff as appropriate. Regardless of the size of the business, the key principles of crisis management still hold true and there is often much more at stake in terms of business survival for smaller businesses.

Arrangements for covering the cost of a recall

Even if an insurance policy is in force to cover costs, these funds may not be available for some time after the event. As a recall could be extremely costly, it is important for suitable funds to be readily available so that the necessary actions are not hampered by concerns about money when time will be of the essence.

Record keeping

It is important for accurate chronological records to be kept of the events throughout a product recall and of the basis of decision-making. It may be necessary to make crucial decisions with only partial or incomplete information being available, which with the benefit of hindsight may appear inappropriate. Records will not only aid the post-recall evaluation but, importantly, will help to demonstrate a 'due diligence' statutory defence in the event of legal proceedings being contemplated against the company (see Chapter 4, for further details on the due diligence defence).

Under the Food Safety Act 1990, a food authority may not begin a prosecution after three years have elapsed from the commission of the offence. Records should be retained for a period exceeding the shelf life of the product but for a minimum of five years, to allow for delays in the case being heard. It should be noted that civil actions for damages with respect to personal injury may not normally be brought after the expiry of three years from the date that the claimant was aware that he had grounds for an action.[3]

Data on suppliers

Accurate details should be maintained of all suppliers of food and food contact materials, including the product supplied, quantity and lot/consignment details. In addition, contact details such as name of contact person, telephone number, fax number and e-mail should be maintained and reviewed for accuracy at three-monthly intervals.

Production records

Accurate details of total production volume of each product should be readily available, together with information on which constituents or ingredients were used to make up each batch of production. The storage and distribution records should be such that the current location of each batch within the food supply chain can be easily identified.

Distribution records

Up-to-date records of trade customers should be maintained in order to identify and notify them of any suspect products that may be in their possession. Sales records should be able to identify the product supplied, quantity and lot/consignment details. In addition, details such as name of contact person, telephone number, fax number and e-mail should be maintained and reviewed for accuracy at three-monthly intervals.

In order to aid a speedy response from suppliers and customers, it would be prudent to inform them of your product recall arrangements and to agree a procedure for the rapid exchange of information in the event of an emergency, including out-of-hours contact details.

Contact details for the food authority, the FSA, Police and the media

Up-to-date contact details should be maintained and regularly reviewed for the local food authority and the Food Standards Agency in the event that notification becomes necessary. Additionally, arrangements for contacting the police should be agreed in advance in the event of malicious product tampering, actual or threats of extortion and blackmail concerning food products. As a general guide, in life-threatening situations arising from malicious product tampering, extortion or blackmail, the police should be contacted by dialling '999' for an emergency response. In non-life threatening cases, advice should be sought from a 24-hour helpline operated by the National Criminal Intelligence Service (NCIS). See the Useful Contacts at the end of this book for further contact details

The NCIS may then liaise with the food company and relevant bodies such as government departments, the Food Standards Agency and food authorities in accordance with agreed protocols. The recall plan should also include up-to-date contact details for local and national media such as television companies, radio stations and newspapers.

Mechanism for recalling product

In order to facilitate a rapid response to a food emergency situation, the Recall Plan should include some templates of product recall notices in the form of standard letters, fax messages and sample press releases that may be quickly completed or adapted to suit the particular circumstances.

Logistical arrangements

Where the potential product recall is likely to be large-scale, arrangements should be made to ensure that suitable staff resources will be available to deal with enquiries and to make contact with suppliers or customers, including out of business hours. Such personnel should be suitably trained to perform their task. If the services of an external public relations company are to be used, a list of vetted and approved companies should be readily available, together with contact details.

The recall 'control centre' venue should be large enough for the purpose and be suitably equipped with the necessary hardware with respect to telephone lines, fax machines and information technology.

Recalled product

The recall plan should include detailed instructions on what is to be done with the recalled product. Once the product is returned to the retailer or the seller, arrangements should be in place for its transport to a designated place, which for temperature sensitive products should include refrigerated transport and storage. For potentially large recalls, where the company's own warehousing capacity is likely to be exceeded, it will be necessary to make arrangements with external warehouses in advance. All recalled product should be quarantined and clearly labelled to prevent it being inadvertently used for an unauthorised purpose.

While the decision of the recall team on the final destination of the recalled product will be dictated by the precise circumstances, the initial question to be addressed is its fitness for human consumption. In some cases where the product has been shown to be contaminated or defective, there may be no option other than to destroy it in order to remove it from the food supply chain. Where the recall is conducted under uncertain circumstances or purely as a precaution and the product's fitness for human consumption has not been determined, further tests or laboratory analysis may be necessary to enable a decision to be made on the future of the recalled product. In some cases, for example where the product is perfectly fit for human consumption but the recall was made due to mislabelling or some reason other than unfitness, the product may be returned to the supply chain once the defect has been corrected, possibly after some rework.

Where the product is known to be unfit for human consumption, it may be suitable for use as pet food or animal feed, possibly following further processing. It is vitally important for accurate records to be maintained of the recalled product and its final destination, not only to enable the success of the recall to be evaluated but to ensure that food unfit food human consumption is not returned to the human food supply chain. Following some high-profile incidents of fraud involving unfit meat being returned to the human food supply chain, food businesses should exercise extreme vigilance in ensuring that recalled products deemed to be unfit for human consumption do indeed reach their intended destination.

Where the product is subject to an investigation by a food authority or the Food Standards Agency, it is quite possible that it could be formally detained pending further tests and in some cases seized and brought before a Justice of the Peace. Whether the decision to destroy the product is taken by the company or imposed by a Justice of the Peace, arrangements should be in place for its destruction or disposal. If a claim is to be made against an insurance policy, due consideration should be given to the insurance company's requirements. It is likely that a representative of the insurance company will need to examine the product personally or require some form of independent verification of the type and quantity of product lost, together with evidence of the cause of loss.

Simulation exercises

Once the recall plan has been formulated, periodic simulation exercises should be conducted to test the system, which should involve all the relevant personnel, both internally and at different stages of the food supply chain. As mistakes in implementing the plan could be extremely costly and damaging for the business, such exercises are invaluable in highlighting shortcomings so as to enable the plan to be fine-tuned.

Recall procedure

The recall procedure consists of a series of logical steps from receiving information on a potential food recall, implementing a recall through to conducting a post-recall assessment. Once the criteria for a potential recall is satisfied as part of the food complaint handling procedure, the recall co-ordinator should be notified immediately. He should in turn conduct an initial assessment of the risk of injury or illness to consumers and the likelihood of damage to the company brand or reputation arising from the food complaint.

If a product recall is not warranted, the matter should be dealt with as a normal complaint through established procedures. If, however, it appears to the recall co-ordinator that a potential recall situation exists, the product recall procedure should be triggered starting with the first step of convening a meeting of the recall team.

Steps 1 to 9 below detail the recall procedure from beginning to end, while a flow chart of key actions to be taken, is shown in Figure 6.1.

Step 1 – Convene recall team

Once the team is convened, as much relevant information as possible should be collated to aid the decision-making process, for example the nature and extent of the potential hazard. The recall coordinator should ensure that each team member understands his/her role, particularly those with responsibility for obtaining relevant information.

Step 2 – Risk assessment

Having collated all the information available, an assessment of the risk of injury or illness should be carried out by evaluating the seriousness of the health hazard and the likelihood of the hazard being realised. In doing so, the following factors should be considered:

- whether there is evidence of actual injury or illness from the consumption of the food in question;
- whether any particularly vulnerable groups in the community, such as children, the elderly or immuno-compromised individuals, are at risk;
- assessment of the degree of seriousness of the health hazard to which consumers would be exposed;
- assessment of the likelihood of the occurrence or risk of the hazard;
- assessment of the consequences (immediate or long-term) of occurrence of the hazard or severity.

It should now be possible to assign a classification to the recall. In the absence of an internationally recognised system, the United States Department of Agriculture (USDA)[4] classification system is considered to be the most appropriate. This is detailed as follows:

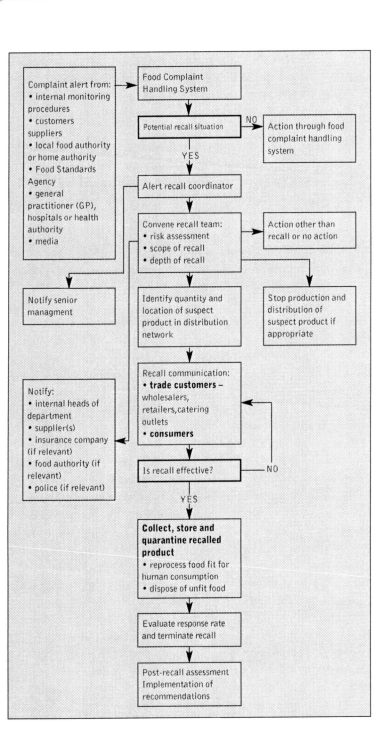

Figure 6.1
Recall procedure

Class 1 – This is a health hazard situation where there is reasonable probability that the use of the product will cause serious, adverse health consequences or death. For example, the presence of pathogens such as E.coli O157 or Clostridium botulinum in food.

Class 2 – This is a health hazard situation where there is a remote probability of adverse health consequences from the use of the product. For example, the presence of undeclared allergens such as milk or soya products.

Class 3 – This is a situation where the use of the product will not cause adverse health consequences. For example, the presence of undeclared, generally recognised as safe non-allergen substances, such as excess water.

If the reason for the recall is a commercial one, for example to protect the brand, a similar risk assessment process should be used to evaluate the nature and severity of the harm to the company from the threat to the brand, perhaps from adverse publicity and the subsequent impact on the market share.

Step 3 – Scope of recall

At this stage it is necessary to determine what products should be recalled. If the hazard is only associated with known batches of production or consignments, it should be relatively easy to limit the scope. Where insufficient information is available, the recall team must decide on the criteria to be used in deciding which type and quantity of product is to be recalled but it would be useful to refer to the HACCP documentation for the process in question.

If the cause of the recall is product contamination during production, a good starting point is all products covered by a single HACCP plan. This could, however, extend to several product types if a generic HACCP plan is used. While the final decision will be dictated by the exact circumstances at the time of a recall, all product batches produced between successive hygiene shifts could be included. At this stage the ability to identify products by the product coding system is critical, in addition to the system of tracing the finished product back to raw materials. Where such records are not available or cannot be relied upon, there will be no choice but to recall complete batches of production, including those in perfect condition.

Step 4 – Depth of recall

From the information on the scale and severity of the food hazard it should be possible to evaluate which products are implicated and how far along the food supply chain they have been distributed. This should enable the recall team to decide the depth of the recall.

If distribution records for the products in question show that they have been despatched to customers and traced to distribution centres, wholesale outlets, retailers or catering premises, the recall can be limited to the trade only, which should be relatively straightforward. If, on the other hand, the product has already reached the final consumer, then the recall becomes more complex as product retrieval will be more difficult. In either case, the communication strategy must be appropriate to suit the target group in question.

Step 5 – Recall communication

The action taken at this stage will be determined by the particular circumstances and the type of recall but clearly, having assessed the situation, it is critical to communicate information to others. Firstly, senior management within the company should be briefed as well as heads of departments concerned with quality assurance, warehousing/distribution, marketing, sales, manufacturing, finance, legal and public relations. If the cause of the hazard has been identified, appropriate action should be taken from ceasing production of the product to quarantining suspect products under the company's control and preventing further deliveries to customers. If an insurance claim is to be made to cover the cost of the recall, the insurance company should be notified in accordance with policy conditions. In addition, suppliers of the product or raw materials should be notified.

If relevant, the local food authority (home authority) and the Food Standards Agency should also be notified of the details of the recall. Based on information provided by the company and the food authority, in accordance with the Food Safety Act 1990, Code of Practice No. 16, the Food Standards Agency may decide to issue a Food Hazard Warning notification to Food authorities and other interested parties throughout the UK. In the case of actual or threats of extortion and blackmail by individuals or pressure groups of varying descriptions, the police should be notified in accordance with arrangements detailed in the recall plan.

In order to initiate the actual recall of products, the consignees should be contacted in accordance to the risk communication strategy in the recall plan. This will be dictated by the level of recall and the particular circumstances under consideration. A trade recall affecting distribution centres, wholesale outlets and retailers is likely to involve a 'silent recall', whereby the affected product may be recalled without the necessity for notifying any other parties. If the recall extends to the final consumer, this will require consideration of wider factors as discussed below.

Depending on the circumstances, the recall notice should be communicated by telephone, fax, e-mail or special delivery letters in envelopes conspicuously marked URGENT – FOOD RECALL.

Recall communication content
The content of a recall communication is critical in maximising the purpose of the exercise and should be based on the following guidelines:

- Be brief and to the point;
- Identify clearly the product, package sizes, lot numbers, codes and any other pertinent descriptive information to enable accurate and immediate identification of the product;
- Explain concisely the reason for the recall and the hazard involved;
- Provide specific instructions on what should be done with respect to the recalled products; and
- Provide ready means for the recipient of the communication to report to the recalling firm whether it has any of the products, eg by allowing the recipient to place a collect call to the recalling firm.[5]

Where necessary, follow-up communication should be sent to those who fail to respond to the initial recall communication.

Consumer recall notification
Where the product in question has been distributed to the general public,

its retrieval will require considerable coordinated effort on the part of the manufacturer or retailer, not to mention potentially vast expenditure. In order to successfully convey the purpose of a recall communication to the general public, the recall team must decide the most appropriate strategy. This may be through issuing a press release to the general news media (national and local) or through specialised media such as professional, trade or minority ethnic press, notices at the point of sale in stores and, if individual customers can be contacted, through personal communication. In serious cases where there is risk of injury to consumers, it would be prudent to take out prominently placed advertisements in newspapers in addition to issuing press releases. Interestingly, the General Product Safety Regulations 1994[6] extend the powers of the Secretary of State (available under section 13 of the Consumer Protection Act 1987) to serve a 'notice

---

Recall Message Checklist

• Start the recall message in a way everyone will understand – one suggested heading is 'Warning – Important Safety Notice'.

• Say what the product is.

• Tell consumers what may be wrong with the product and what the potential danger is. It is usually inappropriate (and unnecessary) to say what caused the problem, eg quality assurance problem in the factory.

• Give information to help consumers correctly identify the product. State which geographic areas are affected and mention specific retailers or distributors (if appropriate). Give the span during which the product might have been bought and list the batch or serial numbers of products which may be affected.

• Include an illustration or photograph of the product. This helps to show where the potential fault is, and can also indicate where consumers will find batch or serial numbers to tell them if their product may be affected.

• Tell customers what to do, for example stop using it, throw it away, or take it back to the shop for a refund or replacement.

• Tell consumers how they can contact you with extra queries – a freephone telephone number is ideal. Also include your company's name and address. Details of your website, or e-mail address could also be useful.

• Apologise to consumers for any inconvenience caused.

Figure 6.1
Recall message checklist

to warn' on a trader, requiring him, at his own expense, to publish a warning about any relevant goods, including food, that the Secretary of State considers to be unsafe.

The content of the recall message is extremely important and, therefore, care should be taken in ensuring that it will convey the intended message to the target group. The recall message checklist shown in Figure 6.1 is suggested by a Department of Trade and Industry publication on Consumer Product Recall[7]. Although this publication deals with consumer products generally and not food products specifically, the principles are equally applicable.

Step 6 – Check effectiveness of recall communication

Having sent out the recall communication, one should not assume that the message is being implemented, therefore, it is imperative that follow-up checks are carried out with consignees. The purpose of this is to verify that, firstly, they received the notification and secondly, that the recommended action is being implemented.

This process can be made much easier if prior arrangements have been made with the consignee on the recall procedure to be followed, in accordance with the Recall Plan. An accurate record should be kept of all parties contacted and any feedback received, including timescales. This may prove to be extremely useful in demonstrating that the company acted responsibility on the basis of available information.

Step 7 – Response rates and termination of recall

Once feedback is available on the effectiveness of the recall, theoretically it will be possible to calculate the % effectiveness of the exercise by using the following simple formula:

$$\% \text{ effectiveness} = \frac{\text{No. of units returned}}{\text{Total no. of units in circulation}} \times 100$$

It should be noted, however, that this figure must be treated with caution, as it only takes account of the number of units returned. It would not be accurate with respect to consumer recalls as consumers may simply dispose of the product rather than returning it to the retailer, especially where the product has a short life or if it is a low-value product. All relevant parties who participated in the recall should be contacted to inform them of feedback on the effectiveness of the recall and any further action that may be required from them. Having taken steps to deal with the recalled product, which may range from destruction through to possible reprocessing, the recall should be formally terminated by the recall team.

Step 8 - Post-recall assessment

Following the termination of the recall, the recall coordinator should collate comments from team members and compile a detailed report on the whole incident, including cost and effectiveness and lessons to be learnt, together with recommendations for improvements for the future, for presentation to senior management. Where recommendations are made for improving the company's food safety management system, particularly with respect to the HACCP system, any proposed changes should be implemented on the basis of risk assessment and reviewed in accordance with set timescales.

Role of the media

In today's world of global communication networks incorporating satellite technology and the increasing influence of the World-Wide Web, providing consumers with almost instant access to new developments, any modern food business that ignores the power of the media does so at its peril. According to Bland:

> While crisis management is about much more than just handling the media, it is also true to say that they can play the single biggest role in a crisis/opportunity.[8]

One of the key factors to recognise in any crisis management is the way the media operate and to appreciate the pressures and demands that drive journalists. As the whole ethos of the media is driven by the 'commercial imperative' of being able to sell a story to the TV viewer, radio listener or newspaper reader, communicating a message concerning a food emergency that a food business wants to convey will not necessarily coincide with the priorities of the media. In dealing with the media, one must not underestimate the speed with which a story can appear on TV, radio or the Internet.

With the increasing popularity of investigative journalism, media companies are prepared to go to great lengths and spend large sums of money to get a story. This point is graphically illustrated by the current popularity of television programmes showing footage filmed by journalists working undercover in well known restaurant chains and food factories in order to expose examples of poor hygiene practices and even large-scale fraud within the food industry. While no food business can realistically hope to control the media output of their crisis, there are a number of measures that may be implemented to convey the company in as positive a light as possible and to minimise the damage.

Firstly, dealing with the media should form a part of the crisis management system, so that the response may be planned in advance. Secondly, it is critical for the company to nominate a skilled spokesperson with the personality to remain in control under difficult circumstances to be trained in dealing with the media. The communication arrangements within the company should direct all media contacts through to the nominated person or department. Also to ensure consistency in any outgoing messages, this should be channelled through a single spokesperson.

An appreciation of the importance of 'the deadline' for the story to reach the newsroom is likely to reflect positively on the company in the final output from the journalist. Bland suggests that the best way to gain some control over what the media is reporting is 'to be helpful, give them what they want and learn to work together'. In this way, a company may be able to diminish the negative and enhance the positive aspects of the incident.

Where the food emergency involves consumers in other countries, it is important to take national differences into consideration when dealing with the media reports that will be transmitted to those countries. In order to maximise the value of any message, the spokesperson should be able to communicate in such a way as to accommodate the nature of TV and radio reporting through 'sound bites' lasting a few seconds at a time. Ultimately, however, the impact of any news story may well be dictated by the nature of other news stories breaking that day. On a quiet news day, a story about a food emergency or 'scare' is likely to take the lead in the headlines.

It is worth noting that in serious cases, the food authority and/or the Food Standards Agency is likely to issue press releases of their own. The Food Safety Act 1990, Code of Practice No.16 provides guidance to food authorities on dealing with the media. Importantly, the guidance recommends that:

> ... food authorities should liaise as far as possible with other interested parties, for example, the food industry, Home or Originating Authority, or the police, on the content and timing of any media pronouncement ...[10]

In addition, it recommends that.[11]

> ... any business mentioned in a media announcement should be informed beforehand especially in the early stages of an investigation, or should be provided with a copy, whenever possible, in advance of release to the press. Action to protect the public should not, however, be delayed.

A food business implicated in a food emergency should not just wait passively and hope for the best outcome. By actively engaging in any discussions about press releases with the food authority and the Food Standards Agency, the company is much more likely to influence the outgoing message positively.

Notes
1. M. Bland (1998) Communicating Out of a Crisis (Macmillan).
2. ANZFA (2001) Food Industry Recall protocol, 4th edn (ANZFA). Copyright Commonwealth of Australia – reproduced by permission.
3. Limitations Act 1980.
4. FSIS Directive 8081.1, Rev. 3 – Recall of Meat and Poultry Products (2000).
5. FSIS Directive 8081.1, Rev. 3 – Recall of Meat and Poultry Products (2000).
6. SI 1994/2328.
7. DTI (1999) Consumer Product Recall – A Good Practice Guide, URN 99/1172.
8. FSIS Directive 8081.1, Rev. 3 – Recall of Meat and Poultry Products (2000).
9. Enforcement of the Food Safety Act 1990 in relation to the Food Hazard Warning System (HMSO, 1997).
10. Food Safety Act 1990, Code of Practice No. 16 (HMSO).
11. Food Safety Act 1990, Code of Practice No. 16 (HMSO).

Chapter 7
Mechanisms for dealing with food emergencies

The Food Standards Act 1999 places the responsibility and the powers for dealing with food emergencies in the UK with the Food Standards Agency (FSA). While the UK headquarters are in London, national offices are located in Scotland, Wales and Northern Ireland. The FSA is accountable to Parliament through Health Ministers and to respective devolved administrations. In order to enable the FSA to carry out its duties smoothly, the relationship with relevant government departments and agencies is outlined by a series of bilateral concordats. So far such administrative concordats have been agreed with the Department of Health (DH), Department for the Environment, Food and Rural Affairs (DEFRA), Department for Education and Skills, the Public Health Laboratory Service (PHLS), the Local Authority Coordinating Body on Food and Trading Standards (LACORS) and the Health and Safety Executive (HSE).

In the concordats, specific reference is made to the arrangements for dealing with food emergencies, particularly on sharing relevant information. For example, the FSA is responsible for dealing with outbreaks of foodborne infection and food hazards but the Department of Health will deal with non-food related outbreaks of gastro-intestinal infection. The Department of Health will retain responsibility for outbreaks involving water, those related to direct contact with animals or with contaminated environments, for example, Leptospirosis or Weil's disease caused by infected rat's urine, and those arising from person-to-person infection.

The current arrangements for dealing with different types of food emergencies have developed in a gradual manner over a number of decades but in bringing the responsibility within the remit of the FSA, a major step has been taken to towards a consistent, unified and coherent approach.

Food incident team

Food emergencies concerning incidents/emergencies involving contamination of food by micro-organisms, chemicals and foreign bodies during processing and throughout the distribution chain are dealt with by the Food Incident Team of the Local Authority Enforcement Division (LAED) within the Food Standards Agency. This team may be alerted about such incidents by food authorities, the PHLS, health authorities, medical practitioners or food businesses or directly by members of the public.

With respect to food poisoning incidents, the Food Incident Team works closely with the Outbreak Control Team set up by the relevant health authority/food authority in accordance with Department of Health guidelines[1] (or their equivalent in Scotland, Wales and Northern Ireland) on the management of outbreaks of foodborne illness. Where the incident warrants food being taken out of the food supply chain, a Food Hazard Warning may be issued to food authorities and other interested bodies such as the PHLS, LACORS and food industry trade organisations. Approximately one in ten notifications to the Food Incident Team lead to a Food Hazard Warning being issued. (See Chapter 4, p. 39 for a discussion on the Food Hazard Warning system.)

Following consultation with the relevant food authorities and the food business implicated in the Food Hazard Warning, a press release may be issued in order to alert the public of possible public health risks of consuming the food in question. Where the circumstances warrant taking statutory action instead of relying on voluntary procedures, the Food Incident Team is instrumental in instigating and then implementing emergency control measures through provisions of the Food Safety Act 1990 and the Food and Environment Protection Act 1985.

Incident response team

The Incident Response Team of the Radiological Protection and Research Management Division (RPRMD) within the FSA deals with food emergencies arising from chemical or radiological contamination, where the source of the contamination is usually from a fixed location such as a chemical plant or nuclear power station. These incidents may cover large geographical areas of land or sea and may result from fires, chemical/oil spills or radiation leaks. The food in question is usually but not always at the primary production stage, for example crops or food animals on a farm or in a fishing area. Typically the division deals with over 200 incidents a year and consults widely with specialists such as toxicologists and the Pesticide Safety Directorate, while maintaining close links with other government departments, the National Radiological Protection Board (NRPB) and Radiation Incident Monitoring Network (RIMNET).[2]

Under the Nuclear Installations Act 1965, operators of nuclear installations are required to test their emergency arrangements as a condition of their licence. In addition, the Radiation Emergencies Preparedness and Public Information Regulations 2001,[3] place a duty on relevant local authorities to test their off-site emergency plans at intervals not exceeding three years. Prior to the establishment of the FSA, the Radiological Safety and Nutrition Division (RSN) of the Department of Health organised two major exercises with chemical contamination scenarios, namely FOODEX (1996) and POLAX (1998). The FSA regularly participates in multi-agency exercises to ensure that arrangements at both local and national level are appropriate. As emergencies covered by this division tend to be major, not only in severity but also scale, any legal enforcement required is most appropriately taken under the Food and Environment Protection Act 1985, which empowers the Secretary of State (or the FSA by arrangement) to make orders to effectively ring-fence a designated area and/or prevent movement or sale of specified products.

With respect to incidents of environmental contamination, the FSA's primary role is to protect the public from contaminated food and the Agency's specific responsibilities are as follows:

- To determine the level of any contamination in the food chain;
- To take action to ensure that food contaminated to unacceptable levels does not enter the food chain, implementing, as necessary, restriction orders under the Food and Environment Protection Act 1985;
- To provide advice and information to the public;
- To ensure, in conjunction with the Environment Agencies, the safe disposal of contaminated food; and
- To ensure that subsequent recovery arrangements take account of food safety issues.[4]

The FSA is a member of the Chemical and Pipeline Emergency Liaison Group (CAPELG) and the Nuclear Emergency Planning Liaison Group (NEPLG), charged with the responsibility for coordinating plans for responding to chemical and radiological emergencies across various departments.

Dissemination of information to the public

In addition to coordinating the necessary action between food authorities and the food industry following an emergency, the FSA is responsible for issuing guidance to the public on food safety and public health implications. This was acknowledged by the Joint Food Safety and Standards Group (JFSSG) as being a key responsibility. The following is an extract from the JFSSG's policy document on controlling major food emergencies:

> Effective emergency response will be a key indicator of FSA's performance to the public and to Ministers.[5]

In its Statement of General Objectives and Practices,[6] the FSA clearly sets out that protecting the health of the public and the interests of the consumers in relation to food is the primary aim. This, together with a commitment to operate in an 'open and transparent way', in addition to providing 'clear, practical advice, information and other forms of assistance to all stakeholders', is intended to keep the public informed of all public health issues with respect to food.

Food industry's dilemma

As the food producer may be the first to become aware of a serious hazard associated with his product through his own monitoring procedures or consumer complaints, he will be faced with crucial decisions as to whether he notifies his enforcing authority, the Food Standards Agency and his customers for fear of serious consequences. Willett[7] argues that, in the absence of a general legal duty on the producer to notify the enforcing authority (with the exception of regulations made in response to a number of 'vertical' directives such as the Meat Products (Hygiene) Regulations 1994 (as amended),[8] the potential negative publicity and penalties under both criminal and private law discourage the producer from alerting the authorities.

Unlike the United States of America, Australia, New Zealand and Canada, where the food industry is subject to a mandatory requirement to notify the regulatory authorities of serious risks to consumer safety and recall suspect food, there are no such obligations on the UK food industry. Further, to ensure the smooth withdrawal or recall of suspect food, the United States Department of Agriculture, the Canadian Food Inspection Agency and the

Australia New Zealand Food Authority (ANZFA) issue detailed guidance on product recall procedures to food businesses. While the FSA and food authorities should, in accordance with Food Safety Act 1990, Code of Practice 16, follow the recommended protocol in response to food emergencies, there is no such universally accepted mechanisms or procedures in place for food businesses to follow. It is safe to assume that large-scale food manufacturers and multiple retailers are more likely to implement planned crisis management systems. Also they will invariably have access to guidelines issues by trade organisations such as the British Retail Consortium (BRC) or the Food and Drink Federation (FDF). However, this is not the case for the majority of the food industry, made up of small to medium-sized businesses.

In the absence of any general requirement to notify regulatory authorities under UK legislation and the lack of a clear protocol from the Food Standards Agency or government with respect to dealing with food emergencies, food businesses face a dilemma on whether to notify enforcement authorities of serious food hazards. As discussed in Chapter 8, p.122, the implementation of the General Food Law Regulation,[9] requiring food businesses to notify the competent authority of food placed on the market that may be injurious to health, is intended to remove this dilemma by making a mandatory duty.

Food emergencies across international boundaries

In view of the large amount of food imported into and exported out of the United Kingdom, the likelihood of food emergencies affecting more than one country has increased. Within the European Union and states falling within the scope of the EEA Agreement,[10] the Rapid Alert System for Food and Feed (RASFF) applies. This is operated by Directorate General for Consumer Health and Protection of the European Commission, in order to facilitate the rapid transfer of information on food safety issues that present a serious risk to public health.

The creation of the single market within the European Union (EU) has meant that food supplies can circulate freely throughout the 15 Member States and be available to more than 300 million consumers. With the planned enlargement of the EU to include more and more Member Countries, the potential market for food is set to grow significantly. The rapid alert system has been in existence across the European Community since 1978 and over time, this has developed to reflect the changes brought about by the principles of operating a single market. On 29 June 1992, the system was incorporated into the Council Directive 92/59/EEC on the General Safety of Products[11] and the legal basis of the rapid alert system was provided by Article 8. This directive applies to all consumer products and is not limited to food.

Key principles of the system are to enable the rapid exchange of information between participating Member Countries in the event of a serious and immediate risk to the health of consumers. At a practical level, where any Member State becomes aware of a serious and immediate risk that is likely to extend beyond its own territory, it should immediately inform the European Commission through the established arrangements. In particular, the notifying Member State should provide information on the following:

- information to identify the product concerned;
- the hazard involved, including results of any tests/analysis to assess the level of risk posed;
- the nature of the measures taken or decided on; and
- information on the supply chains where such information is available.[12]

Provided the information is in line with the notification criteria and if necessary, after verifying any details with the notifying country or the country thought to be the source of the food, the Commission will forward it to all Member States by e-mail. The notification will be sent directly to the designated competent authority in each member country, which for the UK is the Food Standards Agency (Food Incident Team). In 1998 the team received 240 notifications through this system, representing a threefold rise from the previous year. The Agency is charged with investigating the incident and taking any appropriate action through the Food Hazard Warning system or, if necessary, by means of relevant statutory measures. Although outside of the RASFF system, the Commission's protocol includes informing the competent authorities in third countries through diplomatic channels where a suspect food product has been exported outside of the rapid alert network or if it has originated from the third country.

Alerts from the Commission will be in the form of a Warning Notification, or Information Notification or as News, depending on the circumstances:

- *Warning Notifications* inform the Member States of risks arising from food already in circulation and require immediate action to remove it from the market.
- *Information Notifications* are used to pass on information on food safety matters, which may be of use to Member States, but may not necessarily warrant any action.
- *News* is a type of communication used to convey general information on international food safety matters that the Commission has become aware of and considers would be useful to Member States.

The Commission may, under exceptional circumstances, carry out its own investigation and/or convene the appropriate committee to discuss the matter in more detail. On receiving the notification, the Member State is required to make appropriate enquiries and without delay contact the Commission with information on whether the product in question has been marketed within its territory, any additional information to enable an assessment of risk posed and any measures taken or decided on. If the product is located within its jurisdiction and no measures have been taken or decided on, the relevant competent authority must inform the Commission of the reasons for this decision.

Even though the rapid alert system has operated for a decade, a number of deficiencies existed with respect to dealing with food emergencies and these were highlighted by an incident originating in Belgium in 1999, involving dioxin contaminated animal feed, leading to concerns over the safety of food. Firstly, the rapid alert system did not apply to animal feedstuffs, contamination of which caused the dioxin crisis. Secondly, the system was limited to the 15 EU Member Countries, Norway, Liechtenstein and Iceland, whereas the dioxin incident affected many third countries around the world. These shortcomings contributed to a review of the system for exchanging information between countries by the European Commission, as a part of wider changes to European food law, culminating in the adoption of the General Food Law Regulation of the European Parliament and of the Council of 28 January 2002.[13]

While the purpose of this Regulation is to address many food safety issues by means of wholesale changes to the way food law is enforced within the EU and Member States have until 1 January 2007 to implement some measures, a number of important provisions with respect to food emergencies have been in force since 21 February 2002. The key control measures already in force are as follows:

• The Rapid Alert System for Food and Feed is extended to include the notification of a direct or indirect risk to human health deriving from food or feed.

• Member States must notify the Commission of any measures they take in order to restrict the placing on the market or where they force the removal from the market by way of withdrawal or recall of any food or feed in order to protect human health and that requires rapid action.

• Member States must notify the Commission of any agreements that Member States come to with food companies which result in restrictions being placed with respect to food or feed due to a serious risk to human health.

• Member States must notify the Commission of any incident where any food or feed has been rejected at a border post by a competent authority.

• Where investigations reveal that suspect food or feed has been exported to a third country, the Commission must provide information to the competent authority in that country.

• Provision has been made for the rapid alert system to be opened to participation by third countries and international organisations by means of agreements with the European Community.

• Member States should respect the confidentiality of commercial information that they become aware of as a result of operating the system, except for information that must be made public to protect human health.

• The Commission has been provided with the power to take emergency measures with respect to food or feed that is likely to constitute a serious risk to human health, animal health or the environment, regardless of whether it originates from Member States or third countries. Where the Commission fails to take emergency measures, even after being officially informed by a Member State, that country is entitled to adopt interim measures, provided it informs the Commission and other Member States.

• The Commission has been charged with setting up a crisis unit and, in cooperation with the European Food Safety Authority, for drawing up a general plan for crisis management with respect to the safety of food and feed.

• While responsibility for coordinating the rapid alert system remains with the Commission, the European Food Safety Authority will be required to assist in any way it can to enable decisions to be made according to the principles of risk analysis.

• The rapid alert system excludes radiological emergencies as defined by Council Decision 87/600/Eurotom.[14]

• As these changes in European food law have been introduced in the form of a regulation, this will ensure uniform implementation across all Member States and allow more transparency. Further, any changes that need to be incorporated to take account of technical and scientific developments in the future may be implemented quickly.

In order to facilitate exchange of information between Member States of the EU on routine food control matters under Article 6 of the Additional Food Control Measures Directive 93/99 EEC, the Local Authorities Coordinating Body on Food and Trading Standards (LACORS) has been designated as the UK liaison body. The purpose of this arrangement is to provide a forum for exchange of information and for administrative assistance to be provided to food authorities in the UK and other EU Member States with respect to food related matters. As the guidance in Food Safety Act 1990, Code of Practice No.20[15] clearly sets out, any serious food safety matters likely to pose a risk to public health, including food emergencies, should be reported directly to the FSA.

Role of the Codex Alimentarius Commission

The Codex Alimentarius Commission (CAC), made up from representatives of the Food and Agriculture Organisation of the United Nations (FAO) and the World Health Organisation (WHO), is responsible for implementing the Joint FAO/WHO Food Standards Programme, the stated aim of which is to protect consumers and ensure fair practices in the food trade. Since its inception in 1961, the CAC has developed into a single international reference point on scientifically based food standards, guidelines and recommendations with respect to ensuring consumer protection. The CAC is based in Rome and comprises 165 member nations, representing some 98 per cent of the world's population. The significance of the Codex Alimentarius (meaning 'food code') was highlighted by the United Nations Resolution 39/248 in 1985, which adopted guidelines for the elaboration and reinforcement of consumer protection. These guidelines advise that:

> ... Governments should take into account the need of all consumers for food security and should support and, so far as possible, adopt standards from the FAO/WHO's Codex Alimentarius ...

With the increasing importance of the international trade in food, estimated to be US$300 – 400 billion per annum, the role played by the CAC in setting standards has come to be regarded as crucial in removing trade barriers and enabling the free movement of food across international boundaries. The General Agreement on Tariffs and Trade (GATT) has been in existence since 1947 and provides the rules for world trade. However, it was not until 1995 at the Uruguay Round of GATT, that the World Trade Organisation (WTO) was established and with the recent membership of China, it now accounts for well over 90 per cent of world trade.

In order to prevent Member States placing unnecessary barriers against international trade, the WTO adopted the Agreement on the Application of Sanitary and Phytosanitary Measures (SPS) and the Agreement on Technical Barriers to Trade (TBT). This meant that members could take measures to protect the environment, human and animal health and protect the consumer at the expense of free trade, provided it was in accordance with the Agreements. The importance of the Codex Alimentarius Commission was further enhanced by the SPS Agreement citing Codex standards, guidelines and recommendations as preferred international measures for facilitating the international trade in food. This has resulted in Member States adopting Codex general principles into their national food legislation. Within the European Union, the Codex Alimentarius has made a significant impact on the development of food law for many years, for example the incorporation of Hazard Analysis and Critical Control Point (HACCP) principles into Council Directive 93/43/EEC,[16] which were later reflected in UK regulations. In the recasting of European food law,[17] key measures such as risk analysis and the precautionary principle have been included to reflect the Codex Alimentarius guidance. In a further shift towards the Codex Alimentarius Commission's approach, the European food law framework currently favours 'horizontal' provisions that apply generally across the food industry, in preference to previous 'vertical' measures that were limited to a specific type of food, for example, meat or dairy products.

The Codex Alimentarius and food emergencies

With respect to minimising the impact of international food emergencies, the Codex Alimentarius Commission produced *Guidelines for the Exchange of Information in Food Control Emergency Situations* in 1995.[18] These guidelines set out the arrangements for the exchange of key information between Member States on the identification of situations where the consumption of certain foods may lead to a risk of serious untoward health effects. Each country is required to identify a primary contact point for food control emergency situations and the Annex to the Guidelines provides a standard format for the exchange of information between importing and exporting countries on the following:

- the nature of the hazard, eg microbiological, chemical or physical;
- Identification of foods concerned;
- action taken to reduce or eliminate the hazard; and
- contact point for further information.

The incident involving dioxin contamination of food and feedstuffs from Belgium in 1999 highlighted a number of shortcomings in these arrangements in that the existing system failed to ensure the rapid exchange of information between affected countries. As a result, the Codex Alimentarius Commission is reviewing the existing arrangements and considering proposals for updating them, submitted by the Australian delegation in conjunction with the Governments of Japan, the Netherlands, the US and the European Commission.[19]

One of the most important proposals is the application of risk analysis principles to emergency situations. This enables the decision-making process for evaluating risk to consumers to be based on a structured approach of risk analysis comprising three components, namely risk assessment, risk management and risk communication. However, it is recognised that in circumstances where adequate information on the emergency situation is not available or where uncertainty exists hindering the risk assessment process, provisional risk management measures may be applied. These should then be reviewed in the light of new information emerging and amended accordingly.

In addition to risk analysis, the proposals elaborate on the methods of communicating information rapidly by telephone, fax or e-mail and on the responsibilities of exporting and importing countries. New proposals are put forward on information to be notified on the level of distribution of the suspect food throughout the food supply chain to aid the risk management process, as well as measures for tighter controls over the re-export of food, once it has been rejected by a country. Finally, in order to keep the FAO and the WHO informed of international food emergencies, it is proposed that they should be provided with copies of the relevant information.

Notes

1. DOH (1994) Management of Outbreaks of Foodborne Illness (Department of Health).
2. JFSSG (1999b) Planning the FSA Response to a Major Food Emergency, CP(99)38/3.
3. SI 2001/2975.
4. FSA (2002)
5. JFSSG (1999b).
6. FSA (2000) Statement of General Objectives and Practices – Putting the Consumer First (FSA).
7. C. Willett (1992) 'The law's role in the emergency control of food', Journal of Business Law, 150.
8. SI No. 3082.
9. EC 178/2002 Laying down the general principles and requirements of food law, establishing the European Food Safety Authority and laying down procedures in matters of food safety. OJ L31/1, 1.2.2002.
10. Norway, Liechtenstein and Iceland.
11. Adopted on 29 June 1992, OJ L228, 11.8.1992, p. 24.
12. Brunko et al. (2002) Rapid Alert System for Food Products in the European Union and Its Possible Extension to Other Countries in the Region, Conference paper, PEC 10/08, FAO/WHO.
13. EC 178/2002, OJ L31/1, 1.2.2002.
14. OJ L371, 20.12.1987, p. 76.
15. Food Safety Act 1990, Code of Practice 20 – Exchange of Information between Member States of the EU on Routine Food Control Matters (HMSO).
16. Of 14 June 1993 on the Hygiene of Foodstuffs, OJ L175, 19.7.1993, p. 1.
17. EC 178/2002, OJ L31/1, 1.2.2002.
18. CAC/GL 19-1995 (FAO/WHO).
19. Codex Committee on Food Import and Export Inspection and Certification Systems, Tenth Session, 2002.

Chapter 8
The future

Having discussed some shortcomings in the existing arrangements within the UK and at the international level, this final chapter looks ahead to the likely developments in the law and mechanisms for dealing with food emergencies in the future, together with their impact on the food industry.

A number of major international food emergencies such as the BSE crisis originating in the UK and widespread contamination of animal feed/food products with dioxin in Belgium highlighted the potential for a large number of consumers to be placed at risk throughout Europe and beyond. These incidents also demonstrated the weaknesses in the law and mechanisms for protecting consumers. In adopting the General Food Law Regulation,[1] the European Community has signalled a strong desire to protect its citizens from risks to their health from food and feed failing to meet safety requirements, while ensuring the proper functioning of the internal market. With particular reference to the prevention and control of food emergencies, a number of measures have been implemented already, such as changes to the rapid alert system, new emergency powers for the European Commission and the establishment of the European Food Safety Authority, as discussed in Chapter 7. In addition, provision has been made for a range of further measures designed to address food and feed safety risks by means of a structured approach based on risk analysis, although the transition period for implementation for some of these does not expire until 1 January 2007.

Having chosen to provide a high level for protection of human life and health, it is intended that any measures that restrict the freedom of movement of goods within the internal market should be based on a scientific approach. Also, by introducing transparency into the decision-making process, it is hoped that consumer confidence in regulatory authorities and the food industry will be improved. The following sections represent a number of key developments that are likely to affect the way food emergencies are handled in the future.

European Food Safety Authority

This Authority, based on the UK Food Standards Agency model, formally commenced its operation on 1 January 2002 but in practice it will take some months for the various bodies to be appointed, starting with the Management Board. Regulation (EC) 178/2002 sets out the Authority's remit, functions and responsibilities.

According to its remit, the European Food Safety Authority will act as the independent scientific point of reference with respect to risks that have a direct or indirect impact on food and feed safety. In order to enable the risk assessment process to take place, it will commission research and collect and analyse data from relevant sources on emerging risks. Having evaluated the risks, it will communicate this to the European Community institutions and Member States.

The Authority will provide scientific and technical support to the European Commission and Member States in dealing with food emergencies. In the European Commission's White Paper on Food Safety,[2] it was proposed that the responsibility for operating the rapid alert system for food emergencies should rest with the European Food Safety Authority rather than the Commission; however, this did not materialise in the regulation. This means that the European Commission will continue to be responsible for the risk management function of any emergency situation, which may involve enforcement measures, while the European Food Safety Authority will provide support and assistance as necessary. By separating the risk management function of the European Commission, the integrity of the Authority's risk assessment responsibilities and its independence will be preserved.

Risk analysis (Article 6)[3]

The principles of risk analysis with respect to the international trade in food were developed by the Codex Alimentarious Commission. The motivation for this came from the increasing importance of food in international trade and the desire of the World Trade Organisation to prevent unjustified barriers to trade between Member Countries. However, it is recognised that in some circumstances, Members should be entitled to take measures that conflict with the free movement of goods, provided these comply with adopted Agreements. Article 5(1) of the Agreement on Sanitary and Phytosanitary Measures (SPS) provides that:

> Members shall ensure that their sanitary and phytosanitary measures are based on an assessment, as appropriate to the circumstances, of the risk to human, animal or plant life and health, taking into account risk assessment techniques developed by the relevant international organisations.

In this context, the relevant international organisation is the Codex Alimentarius Commission. At its 22nd Session in 1997, the Commission adopted a Statement of Principle[4] relating to the role of Food Safety Risk Assessment, which states, inter alia, that:

> ... health and safety aspects of Codex decisions and recommendations should be based on a risk assessment, as appropriate to the circumstances ... and ... food safety risk assessment should be soundly based on science, should incorporate the four steps of the risk assessment process and should be documented in a transparent manner ...

Following on from this position, the Commission developed Working Principles for Risk Analysis,[5] setting out the primary purpose as being the protection of the health of consumers and detailing how the principles should be implemented. Risk analysis comprises three distinct components, namely risk assessment, risk management and risk communication. Each of these elements is explored further in the following text.

Risk analysis principles have been wholeheartedly adopted and applied to food law by the European Community. By virtue of Article 6 of the General Food Law Regulation[6], provision is made for:

> ... food law to be based on risk analysis except where this is not appropriate to the circumstances or the nature of the measure ...

Also, risk assessment must be based on scientific evidence and carried out in an independent, objective and transparent manner. Where uncertainty exists or decisions have to be made on the basis of incomplete information being available, it is accepted that Member States should have the right to take provisional risk management measures. However, these measures should be reviewed in the light of scientific evidence becoming available within a reasonable period of time and the measures taken should be proportionate to the risk. This is known as the 'precautionary principle'.

Member States are required to adapt existing food law to incorporate the general principles of food law and of transparency in the new regulation, including risk analysis, the precautionary principle, protection of consumer interests, public consultation and public information, as soon as possible but no later than 1 January 2007. However, until these provisions are incorporated by means of domestic legislation, these principles should be taken into account in implementing existing legislation. Interestingly, the regulation defines some key terms with respect to risk analysis, as follows:

> *Risk assessment* – a scientifically based process consisting of four steps: hazard identification, hazard characterisation, exposure assessment and risk characterisation.

> *Risk management* – the process, distinct from risk assessment, of weighing policy alternatives in consultation with interested parties, considering risk assessment and other legitimate factors, and, if need be, selecting appropriate prevention and control options.

> *Risk communication* – the interactive exchange of information and opinions throughout the risk analysis process as regards hazards and risks, risk-related factors and risk perceptions, among risk assessors, risk managers, consumers, feed and food businesses, the academic community and other interested parties, including the explanation of risk assessment findings and the basis of risk management decisions.

The precautionary principle (Article 7)[7]

This principle has attracted much attention due to its importance in enabling the smooth functioning of the international trade in food. As a principle, it was first recognised in the World Charter for Nature adopted by the United Nations General Assembly in 1982 and later enshrined into the Rio Declaration at the UN Conference on the Environment and Development (UNCED) in Rio de Janeiro in 1992.

The importance of the precautionary principle has long been recognised within the European Community and in 2000, the European Commission issued a Communication[8], setting out the Commission's approach to the principle and guidance on its application. The relevance to emergency food controls is clear as any Member State, including the UK, wishing to take enforcement action on the basis of the precautionary principle, that places a restriction on the free movement of goods within the single market must adhere to this guidance. The principle comprises two distinct parts. The first is the political decision by Members States to act or not to act to deal with a perceived risk. If a decision is taken to act, then the second part of the principle is to decide on what action should be taken.

The European Community takes the position that it has the right to establish an appropriate level of protection with respect to the environment, human, animal and plant health. In exercising this right, the precautionary principle is recognised to play an important part, within the structured approach of risk analysis. Where action is deemed necessary, measures based on the precautionary principle should be, inter alia:[9]

- proportional to the chosen level of protection;
- non-discriminatory in their application;
- consistent with similar measures taken already;
- based on an examination of the potential benefits and costs of action or lack of action;
- subject to review in the light of new scientific data; and
- capable of assigning responsibility for producing the scientific evidence necessary for a more comprehensive risk assessment.

In the UK, the Food Standards Agency has published its approach to risk[10] and this largely reflects the European Commission's position on putting the consumer first and taking a precautionary approach; however, where action is taken, this will be proportional to the risk.

Traceability (Article 18) [11]

In response to some major shortcomings brought to light by the dioxin crisis in 1999, the European Community has adopted a key proposal from the European Commission to enable traceability of food, feed, food-producing animals and other substances intended to be or expected to be incorporated into food or feed at all stages of production, processing and distribution. In recognition of the task ahead for the food and feed industry, this requirement does not come into force until 1 January 2005. The practical implication of this requirement is that all operators of the relevant businesses must be able to identify their suppliers and those businesses to which they, in turn, supply their products.

Food or feed will have to be labelled or identified so as to enable traceability and businesses must establish suitable systems for enabling relevant information to be provided to the competent authority on request. In order to allow suspect food, feed (and food-producing animals and other substances intended to be or expected to be incorporated into food or feed) to be traced throughout the food supply chain quickly and efficiently, all businesses along the supply chain will need to be identified. It is likely that each business will be allocated a unique registration number by the relevant competent authority. This number should then accompany the product until its final destination. With respect to food premises in the UK, these are already subject to registration with the food authority by virtue of the Food Premises (Registration) Regulations 1991, therefore, in theory, this should not prove to be too onerous for food authorities to administer.

It is possible that the Food Standards Agency may take this measure to identify food premises a step further and apply the concept of prior approval to food premises more widely than is the case at present. Although the concept is not new and the implementation of 'vertical' directives relating to food of animal origin already require certain types of food premises to be approved, the success of the butchers' shops licensing regulations may prove a significant factor in favour. This is supported by the FSA's announcement, soon after coming into existence.[12] If Licensing is introduced for all food premises, the FSA will be implementing one of the most important recommendations of the Richmond Committee[13] well over a decade ago and fulfilling a long-standing call from organisations such as the Chartered Institute of Environmental Health.

Withdrawal or recall of suspect food/feed (Articles 19/20)[14]

In a measure to be in force throughout the EU no later than 1 January 2005, the food/feed business operator must immediately initiate withdrawal of the food/feed not in compliance with food/feed safety requirements once it has left his immediate control and inform the competent authority. If food/feed has reached the consumer/user, the business operator must take measures to inform the consumer/user of the reason for withdrawal and, if necessary, conduct a recall of the product. Where feed fails to satisfy feed safety requirements, it must be destroyed unless the competent authority is satisfied otherwise.

The food/feed business operator will be under a duty to inform the competent authority immediately, if he considers or has reason to believe that a food or feed which he has placed on the market may be injurious to health or fails to satisfy feed safety requirements respectively. The food/feed business operator will be required to collaborate with the competent authority on action taken to avoid or reduce risks posed by the product they supply or have supplied. Retailers or distributors of the relevant products will be required to take appropriate measures to remove the suspect product from the market and to provide information to the competent authority to enable traceability, where requested.

Similar requirements already exist with respect to butchers' shops subject to licensing in Scotland and to some premises subject to approval under 'vertical' directives. However, the wholesale implementation of these requirements in the UK with respect to all types of food and feed will lead to a fundamental change to the relationship between regulatory authorities and food businesses concerning the exchange of information. These measures will bring the UK in line with existing arrangements for dealing with food emergencies in the United States, Australia, New Zealand and Canada. In future, the significantly enhanced powers of competent authorities will inevitably lead to a review of the existing arrangements which rely largely on voluntary action on the part of the food industry from notifying the authorities of potential food hazards in the first place to implementing measures to remove suspect food from the food supply chain.

Food terrorism

In the wake of terrorist attacks on the United States on 11 September 2001 and the subsequent incidents of bio-terrorism using anthrax organisms, the likelihood of further terrorist activity against the United States and the UK has increased. In view of this experience, the use of food as a vehicle for terrorist action against potentially large numbers of people represents a significant threat.

In the United States, the Food and Drugs Administration (FDA) quickly acknowledged the increased likelihood of food terrorism and issued some practical guidance to the food industry[15] The advice is aimed at all food businesses from manufacturers and importers through to retailers and urges them to review their arrangements for food security. This includes security issues related to employees, raw materials, packaging and finished products. The FDA's efforts on preventing food being used as a part of criminal or terrorist activity has intensified since September 2001. The Bush Administration asked for and duly received from the US Congress increased financial resources for the FDA. As a result, the FDA reinforced its existing regulatory efforts by appointing:

- 210 additional import inspectors to monitor imported food;
- 100 additional inspectors to monitor the domestic US food industry;
- 100 additional technical analysts to cope with the increased number of foods sampled for contamination.

The FDA's powers to deal with food emergencies have been further enhanced by requiring food producers to supply information on traceability in order to minimise risks to food safety. In addition to guidance provided to the food industry, the FDA has been instrumental in offering advice to consumers on minimising risks to their health from suspect food. Consumers have been advised to check any food package or canned food before opening and to look for signs of tampering, as well as any unusual smell, taste or appearance. The public is urged to report any signs of tampering immediately to the regulatory authorities on a 24-hour emergency telephone number or at the FDA's local District Offices. In contrast, the UK Food Standards Agency, government and the European Union have taken a low-key approach and no specific guidance has been issued with respect to food terrorism.

Implications of future legislation for the food industry

Historical case studies and the experience of the last 20 – 30 years shows that food emergencies are inevitable, whether due to accidental contamination or deliberate acts. However, the challenge for the food industry and regulatory authorities is to learn from the past. The implementation of the General Food Law Regulation[16] in full within the UK is likely to have a major impact on the food industry, particularly with respect to the prevention and control of food emergencies. Any such legislation will streamline and tighten regulatory controls and ensure a more consistent approach to emergency situations throughout the European Union. The European Food Safety Authority is charged with seeking out emerging risks to food and feed safety so that preventative action can be taken on a proactive basis. Regulatory authorities such as the European Commission, the UK Food Standards Agency and other competent authorities will be given enhanced powers to bring food emergencies under control rapidly.

In the preamble to the Regulation (paras. 30 and 31), reference is made to placing the primary legal responsibility for ensuring food/feed safety on the food/feed business operator (Article 17). In addition, the European Commission Communication on the Precautionary Principle[17] provides that measures based on the precautionary principle should be, inter alia, 'capable of assigning responsibility for producing the scientific evidence necessary for a more comprehensive risk assessment'. This raises the possibility under some circumstances where a competent authority instigates enforcement measures against a food business under the precautionary principle, of the burden of proof being reversed. In circumstances where, following an assessment of available information, the possibility of harmful effects on health is identified but scientific uncertainty persists, provisional risk management measures may be taken by competent authorities, pending the availability of further scientific information. In such cases, the burden of proving the safety of food may fall on the food business rather than the competent authority having to prove the opposite.

This is not an entirely new concept as it is already applied to new drugs, pesticides and food additives where they are presumed to be hazardous and it is the responsibility of the producer to provide scientific proof of their safety before they are allowed to be marketed. A similar reversal in the burden of proof exists in the Health and Safety at Work etc. Act 1974[18], where a general duty on an employer is qualified by the terms 'so far as is practicable, so far as is reasonably practicable, or to use the best practical means' to do something. By virtue of section 40 of the Act, it is the duty of the accused to prove that it was not practical or not reasonably practicable to do more than was in fact done to satisfy the duty or requirement, or that there was no better practicable means than was in fact used to satisfy the duty or requirement. However, this should be read in the light of provisions of the Human Rights Act 1998 and Article 6 of the European Convention on Human Rights, to which the UK is a signatory, with respect to the right to a fair trial.

The cost of implementing the new measures will largely be borne by the food industry and will undoubtedly be passed on to the consumer. The additional resources for the Food Standards Agency and other competent authorities will probably be financed by general taxation, except where charges are made for any licensing or other prior approval schemes. In terms of readiness of the food industry to implement the new measures, the larger food businesses are much more likely to be in a position to cope, both financially and operationally, than the majority of small to medium-sized businesses. Measures to enable traceability of food and feed are likely to have the greatest impact on manufacturers and processors responsible for production and packaging, while distributors and retailers will need to establish suitable systems capable of tracking and recording consignments of food/feed supplied to them.

On the face of it, the fundamental changes in food law appear to be very much in favour of regulatory authorities and likely to impact seriously on the food/feed industry. However, they also hold out the prospect of some benefits for businesses in the longer term. Firstly, by setting out clear requirements on food/feed businesses to withdraw or recall suspect food/feed and notify the competent authority, the dilemma of whether or not to alert authorities and the uncertainty of the existing position will be removed. Secondly, the principles of transparency, consistency and proportionality in the decision-making process, from the initial decision by a competent authority to take action and then onto the actual action itself being based on risk analysis principles, should provide some assurances to the food/feed industry. Thirdly, if regulatory authorities and the food industry are perceived to be working in accordance with risk analysis principles in an atmosphere of openness, this will improve much needed confidence among consumers and repair some of the damage sustained over many years.

With respect to dealing with food emergency situations, there is an overwhelming case for the development of a protocol agreed by regulatory authorities, LACORS, representative organisations of the food industry and other interested parties. Indeed, there is precedence for this type of industry guide to be made by virtue of Article 5 of Council Directive 93/43/EEC[19]. In this way, both regulatory authorities and the food industry will be working in accordance with a mutually agreed protocol based on the principles of risk analysis with the common aim of protecting the consumer's health.

Notes

1. EC 178/2002 Laying down the general principles and requirements of food law, establishing the European Food Safety Authority and laying down procedures in matters of food safety, OJ L31/1, 1.2.2002.

2. COM(1999)719 Final, Brussels, 12.1.2000.

3. OJ L31/1, 1.2.2002.

4. The Application of Risk Assessment Principles in Codex, ALINORM 97/9 – Rev. 1 (CAC/LIM 21).

5. Risk Analysis: Working Principles for Risk Analysis, CX/GP Fifteenth Session of the Codex Committee on General Principles (FAO).

6. OJ L31/1, 1.2.2002.

7. OJ L31/1, 1.2.2002.

8. Communication from the Commission on the Precautionary Principle, COM(2000)1, Brussels, 2.2.2000.

9. Communication from the Commission on the Precautionary Principle, COM(2000)1, Brussels, 2.2.2000.

10. FSA (2000) Statement of General Objectives and Practices – Putting the Consumer First (FSA).

11. OJ L31/1, 1.2.2002.

12. 'FSA to consider licensing', Environmental Health News, vol. 15, no. 4, 7.4.2000.

13. Richmond, M. Sir (Chairman) (1990) The Microbiological Safety of Food, Parts I and II, HMSO.

14. OJ L31/1, 1.2.2002.

15. www.efsan.fda.gov/~dms/secgnid.html.

16. OJ L31/1, 1.2.2002.

17. COM(2000)1, Brussels, 2.2.2000.

18. Chapter 37.

19. Of 14 June 1993 on the Hygiene of Foodstuffs, OJ L175/1, 19.7.1993.

Appendix 1
Useful contacts

Association of British Insurers

www.abi.org.uk

Australia New Zealand Food Safety
Authority

www.anzfa.govt.nz

British Retail Consortium

www.brc.org.uk

Canadian Food Inspection Agency

www.inspection.gc.ca/english

Codex Alimentarius Commission

www.codexalimentarius.net

Chartered Insurance Institute

www.cii.co.uk

Chartered Institute of
Environmental Health

www.cieh.org.uk

Campden and Chorleywood Food
and Drink Research Association

www.campden.co.uk

Department for the Environment,
Food and Rural Affairs

www.defra.gov.uk

Department of Health

www.doh.gov.uk

Department of Trade and Industry

www.dti.gov.uk

European Food Safety Authority

www.efsa.eu.int

European Union
(Food Safety)

www.europe.eu.int/pol/food/
index_en.htm

European Union Business

www.eubusiness.com

Food and Agriculture Organisation
of the United Nations

www.fao.org

Food and Drugs Administration

www.fda.gov

Food Standards Agency	www.food.gov.uk
Her Majesty's Stationery Office	www.hmso.gov.uk
Health and Safety Executive	www.hse.gov.uk
Institute of Food Safety and Technology	www.ifst.org
Institute of Public Relations	www.ipr.org.uk
Key Note Ltd	www.keynote.co.uk
Leatherhead Food Research Association	www.lfra.co.uk
Local Authority Co-ordinating Body on Food and Trading Standards	www.lacots.org.uk
Local Government Association	www.lga.gov.uk
National Criminal Intelligence Service	Kidnap and Extortion Unit PO Box 8000, London SE11 5EN 020 7238 8418/8169
Public Health Laboratory Service	www.phls.co.uk
Sentinel Safety Solutions Ltd	www.sentinelsafety.co.uk
United States Department of Agriculture	www.usda.gov
University of Reading	www.fst.rdg.ac.uk/foodlaw/links.htm
World Health Organisation	www.who.int/en
World TradeOrganisation	www.wto.org

Appendix 2
References and further reading

Abbott, H. (1991) Managing Product Recall. Pitman Publishing.

Ahmed, S. and Steenson, R. (1996) Is There a Risk to Public Health from Listeria Monocytogenese in Lanark Blue Cheese? Unpublished.

Allan, J.D. (Sheriff) (1995) Sheriff's Decision on the Application under section 9 of the Food Safety Act 1990 by Clydesdale District Council. Sheriffdom of South Strathclyde, Dumfries and Galloway at Lanark.

Australia New Zealand Food Authority (1997) Food Industry Recall Protocol. ANZFA, Commonwealth of Australia.

Bannister, N. (2000) Eau, So Sparkling. The Guardian, Pg.31, 17 June.

Bland, M. (1998) Communicating Out of a Crisis. Macmillan Press Ltd.

Brunko, P. et al (2002) Conference Paper – Rapid Alert System for Food Products in the European Union and its Possible Extension to Other Countries in the Region. FAO/WHO. PEC 01/08.

Codex Alimentarius Commission (1997) Application of Risk assessment Principles in Codex. ALINORM 97/9 – Rev.1 (CAC/LIM 21). FAO.

Codex Alimentarius Commission (2002) Proposed Draft Revision to the Guidelines for the Exchange of Information in Food Control Emergency situation. (CAC/GL 19-1995). Codex Committee on Food Import and Export Inspection and Certification Systems. Tenth Session. FAO.

Codex Alimentarius Commission (1997) Food Hygiene Basic Texts - HACCP System and Guidelines for its Application. Annex to CAC/RCP 1 – 1969, Rev 3, FAO.

Codex Alimentarius Commission (1995) Guidelines for the Exchange of Information in Food Control Emergency Situations. CAC/GL 19-1995. FAO/WHO.

Codex Alimentarius Commission (1999) Principles of Risk Analysis. ALINORM 99/9. FAO.

Codex Alimentarius Commission (2000) Risk Analysis: Working Principles for Risk Analysis. CX/GP Fifteenth Session of the Codex Committee on General Principles. FAO.

Commission of the European Communities (1992) Council Directive 92/59/EEC on the General Safety of Products. Brussels, 29 June. OJ No. L228,11/08/1992 P.0024.

Commission of the European Communities (1993) Council Directive 93/43/EEC on the Hygiene of Foodstuffs. Brussels, 14 June.

Commission of the European Communities (2000) Communication from the Commission on the Precautionary Principle. COM (2000). Brussels, 02.02.2000.

Commission of the European Communities (2000) Draft Regulations. COM (2000) 438 Final. Brussels, 14 July.

Commission of the European Communities (2002) EC 178/2002 Laying down the general principles and requirements of food law, establishing the European Food Safety Authority and laying down procedures in matters of food safety. OJ L31/1 1.2.2002.

Commission of the European Communities (1999) Standing Veterinary Committee – Short Report of the Standing Veterinary Committee (99/18) – Brussels, 2 July.

Commission of the European Communities (1999) White Paper on Food Safety. COM (1999) 719 Final. Brussels, 12 January.

Communicable Disease Surveillance Centre (2000) Reported Food Poisoning Cases in England and Wales. Public Health Laboratory Service.

Cornwell, R. (1985) How the drinks were spiked. Financial Times. Pg. 7, 27 July.

Department of Trade and Industry. (1999) Consumer Product Recall – A Good Practice Guide. DTI.

Doeg, C. (1995) Crises Management in the Food and Drinks Industry. Chapman and Hall.

Dowding, T. (1997) Can we have our cans back? Professional Broking, Pg. 30-31, May.

Dowding, T. (1998) Carrying the Can. Professional Broking, Pg. 43-45, November.

Environmental News Network (1999)
www.enn.com/extras/printer-friendly.asp?storyid=3687. 11 June

Errington, H (1996) www.alma-services.co.uk/cannon/lanarkblue/lanarkblue_009.html

Food and Drugs Administration (2001) Food Producers, Processors, Transporters and Retailers: Food Security Preventive Measures Guidance. Available from: www.cfsan.fda.gov/~dms/secgnid.html [Accessed 10 March 2002].

Food Safety Act 1990 – Code of Practice 4 (1991) Inspection, Detention and Seizure of Suspect Food. HMSO.

Food Safety Act 1990 – Code of Practice 6 (1991) Prohibition Procedures. HMSO.

Food Safety Act 1990 – Code of Practice 7 (Revised 2000) Sampling for Analysis or Examination. HMSO.

Food Safety Act 1990 – Code of Practice 16 (Revised 1997) Enforcement of the Food Safety Act 1990 in relation to the Food Hazard Warning System. HMSO.

Food Safety Act 1990 – Code of Practice 20 (1996) Exchange of Information between Member States of the EU on Routine Food Control Matters. HMSO.

Food Safety (General Food Hygiene) (Butchers' Shops) Amendment (Scotland) Regulations 2000 – Guidance Notes. Available from:

http://www.foodstandards.gov.uk/regulation/but_guide.htm [Accessed 14 May 2000].

Food Standards Agency (2000) Food Standards Agency to reduce Food Poisoning by 20 per cent. FSA Press Release 28 July.

Food Standards Agency (2000) FSA to consider Licensing. Environmental Health News Vol. 15, No. 14, 7 April.

Food Standards Agency (2000) Statement of General Objectives and Practices – Putting the Consumer First. FSA.

Food Standards Agency (2001) Consumer Attitudes to Food Standards. Final Report – COI Ref.4695 Taylor Nelson Sofres plc.

Food Standards Agency (2002) Consumer Attitudes to Food Standards Wave 2. – COI Ref. RS250290. Taylor Nelson Sofres plc.

Food Standards Agency (2002) Traceability in the Food Chain - A Preliminary Study.

Garrity, T. (2000) New Food Hygiene Legislation Announced. Environmental Health Journal, September, Pg. 308-311, Volume 108/09.

Griffiths, J. (1999) UK Food Market – Market Review. Key Note Ltd.

Institute of Food Science & Technology (1999) Dioxin-contaminated poultry feed in Belgium. Available from: http://www.ifst.org/dioxedb.htm [Accessed 15 July 2000]

International Standards Organisation (2000) Guidance on the Documentation Requirements of ISO 9001:2000. ISO.

Jacob, M., Billingham, V.S., Rubery, E. (1989) The Role of the Department of Health in the Microbiological Safety of Food. British Food Journal 91,8.

Joint Food Safety and Standards Group (1999)(1) Major Food Emergencies –The FSA, and its liaison with other parts of Government.

Consumer Panel Secretariat. CP(99)38/2.

Joint Food Safety and Standards Group (1999)(2) Planning the FSA Response to a Major Food Emergency. Consumer Panel Secretariat. CP(99)38/3.

Jukes, D. (2000) Department of Food Science and Technology, University of Reading UK Food Law Cases. Available from: http://www.fst.rdg.ac.uk/foodlaw.htm [Accessed 30 September 2000]

Key Note Ltd (1999) UK Food Market - Market Review.

Key Note Ltd (2001) UK Food Market - Market Review.

LACOTS (1998) Due diligence investigation and the Food Safety Act. LAC 10 98 2.

LACOTS (1999) Food Hazard Warning – Dioxin Contamination of Belgian Poultry and Eggs. Ref. 14/99 2 June plus 8 Updates. Available from: http://www.lacots.org.uk/hazard/belgian.htm [Accessed 15 July 2000].

MAP (1999) Grocery Trade in the 21st Century. Market Assessment Publication Ltd.

Mintel (2000) Special Report: Food Safety. Mintel.

Mortimer, S and Wallace, C (1994) HACCP – A Practical Approach. Chapman and Hall.

Office for National Statistics (1997) ONS Family Expenditure Survey 1996/97.

Oughton, D. and Lowry, J. (1997) Textbook on Consumer Law. Blackstone Press Ltd.

Painter, A. A. (1990) A Guide to the Food Safety Act 1990. Butterworths.

Pennington, T.H. (1997) Report on the circumstances leading to the 1996 outbreak of infection with E.coli 0157 in Central Scotland, the implications for food safety and the lessons to be learned. The Stationery Office.

Pepsi-Cola Company (1993) The Pepsi Hoax: What went right? Pepsi-Cola Public Affairs.

Phillips Report (2000) The Inquiry into BSE and Variant CJD in the United Kingdom. The Stationery Office.

Rawstorne, P. (1990) If One Green Bottle Should Accidentally Fall. Financial Times. Pg.23, 16 February.

Rowell, R. (Ed.) Butterworths Law of Food and Drugs. Vol. 1 – 6 Butterworths.

Summers, J.P. (1997) Listeria Monocytogenes in Cheese – Implications for Food Safety Enforcement. REHIS, Unpublished.

Sumner, J. (1995) A Guide to Food Quality Assurance. Publisher not given, ISBN 0 644 42900 3.

Thompson, K. (1996) The Law of Food and Drink. Shaw and Sons.

Thompson, K. (1997) 'Right of Appeal under the Food Safety Act 1990'. Judical Review, 254.

Unites States Department of Agriculture (2000) FSIS Directive 8081.1 Rev.3 – Recall of Meat and Poultry Products. Available from: http://www.fsis.usda.gov/FOIA/dir/8080.htm [Accessed 16 July 2000]

White Paper (1998) The Food Standards Agency – A force for Change. Cm 3830. The Stationery Office.

Willett, C. (1992) The Law's Role in the Emergency Control of Food. Journal of Business Law 150.